KIM PORTER

Lost Words and Hidden Scars

The Untold Truth Behind the Glamour

Jade Winters

This page is intentionally left blank

Disclaimer

This book aims to respectfully explore the life, legacy, and circumstances surrounding Kim Porter, based on publicly available information, reports, and personal testimonies. While every effort has been made to ensure accuracy, certain interpretations, reflections, and perspectives presented in this book are based on the author's understanding of the events and the individuals involved. The book addresses sensitive topics including personal relationships, public and private challenges, and significant life events. It is not intended to provide a definitive or investigative account of all aspects of Kim Porter's life, particularly regarding her passing, but rather to offer an in-depth examination of her legacy and influence. The author has exercised care in handling these subjects with the utmost respect for Kim Porter and all individuals mentioned. The intent is to honor her memory, while also navigating complex issues that are often subject to different interpretations. The contents of this book should not be construed as making factual claims about any person's involvement in specific events unless otherwise corroborated by established and reliable sources. Readers are encouraged to approach the book with the understanding that certain areas, particularly those concerning private relationships and speculative discussions surrounding Kim's death, are treated with sensitivity and care, and no insinuations are made without due consideration. The author and publisher disclaim any liability arising from potential misinterpretation or misunderstanding of the book's content. This work does not seek to accuse or harm any individual but to respectfully reflect on the impact of Kim Porter's life and the lasting legacy she left behind.

Copyright Page

Title: Kim Porter – Lost Words and Hidden Scars. The Untold Truth Behind the Glamour

Author: Jade Winters © 2024 October - Jade Winters

Table of Contents

Preface 1

The Figure of Kim Porter 1

The Purpose of This Biography 2

The Narrative Approach 4

An Invitation to Readers 5

Chapter 1: Roots in Columbus 7

A Southern City at Heart 7

The Importance of Family and Community 8

Sarah Porter: A Model of Strength 9

Joys and Challenges of Childhood 10

Moments of Carefree Joy and Childhood Dreams 11

A Mother's Support in the Early Years 12

Values of Resilience and Determination 13

A Solid Foundation for the Future 14

Chapter 2: Early Dreams and Moving to Atlanta 16

The Ambition to Move Beyond Columbus 16

First Experiences in Fashion 16

Atlanta: The Gateway to a New World 17

A Competitive Environment and New Challenges 18

Moments of Solitude and Her Mother's Support 19

Initial Contacts and Opportunities in Atlanta's Fashion
Scene 21

Reaching Small Milestones and Fueling the Dream 22

A Clearer Vision of the Future 22

Chapter 3: New Experiences in the Fashion World.......... 24

The First Meeting with a Modeling Agency 24

First Photoshoots: A Transformative Experience......... 24

A World of Appearances and Reality 25

The Challenge of Staying Authentic 26

A Photographer Friend and Valuable Advice 27

The First Major Runway Show: Kim's Heartbeat 28

Criticism and Life Lessons 28

A First Glimpse at the Big City: New York on the
Horizon 29

Chapter 4: Moving to New York: A New Beginning........ 31

The Courage to Leave Atlanta... 31

Life in a New City: The Impact of New York 31

New Contacts and the Fashion Network 32

The First Significant Collaborations 33

The Challenge of Staying Grounded in a Volatile World
.... 34

A New Friendship in the Industry.................................. 34

Glimpses and Opportunities in Manhattan................... 35

A Decisive Step Toward Success 36

Chapter 5: Meeting Al B. Sure! and the Birth of Quincy.. 37

A Life-Changing Encounter 37

An Intense and Passionate Relationship........................ 38

Al's Influence on Her Life and Career 39

A Private Life in the Spotlight.. 40

Kim's Desire to Build a Family 41

The News of Pregnancy: A New Adventure................ 42

The Support of Her Mother and the Significance of This Phase... 43

The Arrival of Quincy: An Incomparable Joy................ 44

The Early Months of Motherhood: Challenges and Discoveries 45

A New Balance Between Professional and Family Life 46

An Inevitable Crisis: The Pain of Separation 47

Chapter 6: A New Relationship with Sean "Diddy" Combs 48

A Meeting Destined to Change the Future 48

A Deep and Conscious Connection 49

A New World of Opportunities and Challenges 49

Building Trust in a Public Sphere 50

Kim's Role as a Guide and Support 51

Kim's Drive for a Stable Family...................................... 52

Diddy's Special Bond with Quincy 52

Growing Together Through Challenges and Compromises 53

A Love That Becomes Part of Public Life 54

Preparing for the Future as a Couple and Family.......... 54

Chapter 7: Christian's Birth and Family Growth 56

A Joyful Announcement: Kim's Pregnancy 56

Diddy's Devotion and Growing Bond with Kim 56

Preparing to Welcome Christian 57

The Birth of Christian: Indescribable Joy...................... 57

Kim's Role as Mother to Quincy and Christian............. 58

Diddy's Role as a Father Figure to Quincy...................... 59

Creating a United, Peaceful Home 59

The Challenges of Managing a Family in the Public Eye
.... 60

Moments of Family Joy and Connection........................ 61

A Bond That Grows Beyond Differences 62

Chapter 8: Temporary Crisis, Reconciliation, and the Birth
of the Twins 63

The Burden of Commitments and Differences 63

Moments of Tension and Misunderstanding 63

A Difficult Decision: Temporary Separation 64

The Discovery of an Unbreakable Bond 65

A New Chapter of Complicity and Stability.................. 66

Kim's Pregnancy Announcement: Two New Lives on
the Way 66

Preparing for the Twins' Arrival 67

The Birth of D'Lila Star and Jessie James: A Dream
Realized.. 68

Facing the Challenge of Raising Four Children 69

Challenges Reemerge 70

Chapter 9: The Final Separation and Co-Parenting with
Diddy.. 72

A Period of Growing Tensions 72

The Decision to Go Separate Ways............................... 72

Coping with the Pain of Separation.............................. 73

A Shared Commitment to the Children......................... 75

Building a New Family Structure 76

A Relationship Founded on Respect and Friendship ... 76

Family Moments of Togetherness 77

Diddy's Commitment as a Present Father 79

Chapter 10: New Opportunities in the Entertainment World 80

A Renewed Professional Drive 80

Collaborations with Prestigious Fashion Brands 81

Entering the World of Television 82

Breakthrough Role on the TV Series Single Ladies 83

Expanding Her Personal Brand 84

Future Ambitions and New Prospects in the Industry. 84

Chapter 11: Balancing Motherhood and Career 86

Being a Single Mother to Quincy, Christian, D'Lila Star, and Jessie James 86

Navigating Co-Parenting Challenges 87

Special Moments of Tenderness with the Twins 88

The Challenge of Managing a Large Family 88

Being a Model of Strength and Resilience 89

A Life Devoted to Family 90

Chapter 12: A Guiding Role for Her Children................... 92

Being a Steady Figure for Quincy 92

Encouraging Christian's Artistic Talents 93

Fostering Independence in the Twins 94

Teaching the Value of Authenticity and Integrity 95

Navigating Public Visibility with Her Children.............. 96

Sharing Life Experiences as a Model.............................. 97

Providing Emotional Support at Every Stage 98

Building a Bond Based on Trust and Open
Communication 99

Chapter 13: The Relationship with Diddy: A Lasting
Collaboration 102

A Bond Beyond Separation 102

Co-Parenting as a Priority 103

Shared Celebrations and Important Moments 104

Kim's Support During Diddy's Pressured Moments .. 105

An Inclusive, Extended Family 106

Recognizing Each Other's Contributions 107

Supporting Their Children's Projects and Ambitions . 108

A Model of Respect for Their Children 109

Chapter 14: Public Criticism and Charitable Initiatives .. 112

Life Under the Spotlight 112

Handling Criticism with Grace and Calm 113

Support from Family and Friends 114

Charitable Initiatives as an Expression of Authenticity
.... 115

Balancing Public and Private Life 116

Chapter 15: The Tragedy of Kim's Passing 118

A Day of Pain and Disbelief 118

The Cause of Death and Initial Investigations 119

Grief Among Family and Friends 120

Diddy's Farewell: Words of Love and Remembrance 121

Public Commemoration and Fans' Outpouring of Love
.... 122

An Absence That Changes Everything 123

Chapter 16: Conspiracy Theories and Speculation about Kim Porter's Death 125

The Start of Online Speculation..................................... 125

Statements from Family and Friends............................ 126

The Impact of Conspiracy Theories on Public Opinion 127

The Removal of the Fake Book from Amazon 128

The Importance of Verifying Sources and Respecting the Memory of the Deceased 129

Chapter 17: Diddy's Musical Tribute to Kim Porter in 2023 130

The Decision to Honor Kim Porter at the VMAs 130

An Emotional Performance with Christian "King" Combs 131

Diddy's Words in Memory of Kim................................ 132

The Tribute's Impact on the Audience and Fans 132

A Memory That Continues to Live in Pop Culture 134

Chapter 18: The 2024 Scandal: Diddy's Arrest 136

The Charges and Arrest in New York............................ 136

The Reactions of Kim Porter's Family and Children.. 136

Media Impact and Divided Public Opinion 137

Consequences for Diddy's Career and Project Suspensions 138

Prospects for the Trial and Kim's Legacy..................... 139

Epilogue: Kim Porter's Legacy – A Life That Continues to Inspire.. 140

A Mother's Love and the Legacy of Family 140

A Figure of Resilience and Grace 140

Her Impact on Culture and the Entertainment Industry
.... 141

A Memory That Survives Hardships 142

A Call to Remember Kim for Who She Truly Was 142

UNLOCK
EXCLUSIVE PERKS
INSIDE THE BOOK

Go to page 111
of the Book, and
scan the QR

This page is intentionally left blank

Preface

The Figure of Kim Porter

In the vibrant worlds of fashion and music, few have left a truly lasting and genuine impact like Kim Porter. Her presence transcended beauty and elegance; she embodied a life force that seamlessly combined grace, resilience, and emotional depth. From her early days in the industry, she stood out as an iconic figure, yet her natural charisma was what truly set her apart—a quality that drew not only attention but also the admiration and respect of all who crossed her path.

Kim's career evolved through remarkable phases, from modeling for top brands to taking on roles that demanded a magnetic presence. But her influence extended beyond these pursuits. Those who knew her describe a generous and sincere woman, someone who brought positivity and hope wherever she went. Friends recall how she could light up any room, creating an atmosphere where everyone felt welcome and valued.

Her career and public life were only part of her story. Kim's family, especially her children, was her greatest source of joy and fulfillment. As a mother, she instilled values of authenticity, commitment, and respect in them. Despite the ever-present spotlight, she never let personal success overshadow her family role. Instead, she maintained a careful balance between fame and her private world, proving it was possible to be a respected public figure without sacrificing one's essence.

Close friends share anecdotes of a woman who, no matter how busy, always found time to care for those around her. Kim possessed a rare ability to listen, to understand others' struggles, and to offer heartfelt advice and unwavering support. This empathy became a cornerstone of her life and resonated in all her relationships, both personal and professional. Her presence was cherished and irreplaceable, especially in the often competitive and fast-paced entertainment industry.

Kim's influence transcended the entertainment world, inspiring those who admired her strength and grace under the public eye. Fans saw her as an accessible figure who faced challenges with dignity and integrity. To many, she was an inspiration, proving that one could stay true to oneself even in the limelight. She didn't seek to impress through grand gestures; rather, it was her daily example that conveyed messages of resilience and positivity.

Ultimately, Kim Porter's legacy is one of light and love. Her impact is measured not only in photos or public appearances but in the indelible mark she left on the lives of those who knew her. She remains an example of how to live with intensity, staying true to one's values and bringing a touch of beauty and hope to the world.

The Purpose of This Biography

The decision to write a biography of Kim Porter stems from the desire to tell a rich, nuanced story—one that goes beyond public successes or glamorous images. Kim Porter was not just a public figure; she was a person who deeply touched the lives of others, inspiring those around her and leaving a legacy of humanity and strength in an often-superficial world. This book aims to go beyond the media's portrayal, revealing the complexity of a woman who lived intensely and faced challenges most people will never see.

The main goal is to honor her memory with a faithful, respectful portrayal of her life. Often, when a public figure passes, their story is told with a superficial lens, sacrificing meaningful details in favor of easy stereotypes or sensationalism. In this case, the biography intends to be a work of careful research, a journey that respectfully explores each phase of her life, presenting Kim not just as a celebrity, but as a mother, friend, and resilient woman.

Kim Porter exemplified authenticity in a world where appearances often overshadow substance. Through this biography, we seek to offer readers an honest portrait of who she was, sharing both her brightest and darkest moments without distortion or bias. The choice to tell her story this way is born from admiration for her inner strength and her ability to overcome hardships without losing her identity.

Her life, though marked by significant achievements, was also filled with trials, sacrifices, and tough decisions. This biography seeks to illuminate the human side of Kim, showing her struggle to maintain balance between her public image and her private life. What emerges is the portrait of a woman who faced great challenges with dignity, showing that true strength lies in authenticity and being oneself.

Writing this biography is not only an act of remembrance but also a way to honor the legacy Kim left. Her story encourages us to look beyond appearances, to recognize that behind every smile is a life shaped by choices, hopes, and struggles. This biography serves as a tribute to her journey, a testimony of how Kim turned her experiences into life lessons for all who crossed her path.

In a way, this book is also a message for those living under the spotlight, for those who feel the pressure to meet public expectations. Kim's story shows that it is possible to be authentic and strong, to live with passion without sacrificing integrity. Each chapter of this biography is a piece of the mosaic that makes up Kim Porter's life—a life that deserves to be remembered for its human worth, not just its public image.

The Narrative Approach

In telling Kim Porter's life story, the goal is to go beyond a simple recounting of events. This book takes an approach that combines accuracy with emotional engagement, aiming to capture not only the events of her life but also the emotions, motivations, and thoughts that drove her choices. Each chapter results from careful research, a commitment to gathering and verifying reliable sources, to ensure that what is shared reflects the true story.

The narrative tone strives to be authentic, avoiding sensationalism and honoring Kim's memory. This style reflects the belief that a life so deeply lived deserves to be told with honesty and care, including details often missing from more superficial accounts. Each episode has been chosen to paint a truthful, meaningful picture that reveals the person beyond the celebrity.

This book is not just a tribute but also a reflection on the complexities of a life lived in the public eye. Kim Porter managed to maintain a balance between her public and private worlds, between glamour and personal challenges, and the narration aims to reflect this duality. The episodes follow a chronological line, with special attention to moments that marked a turning point in her life. The narrative focuses on details that reveal Kim's true nature—not only as a style icon but as a determined, sensitive woman who lived with passion and courage.

A biography is not just a list of events but a journey through the experiences that defined a person. In this sense, the approach aims to engage readers, allowing them to immerse themselves in moments of joy, difficulty, and the choices that shaped Kim's path. Each anecdote and testimony has been carefully chosen to provide readers with a full perspective, far from the stereotypes and simplifications often applied to public lives.

The narration also includes realistic details, the product of in-depth, careful research. This work allows room for nuances and hidden aspects that rarely surface in the media's superficial descriptions. Factual accuracy is paired with an empathetic analysis, telling not only what Kim did but also how she felt and approached these experiences emotionally.

The aim is to create a connection between the reader and the story, allowing readers to understand the complexity of the choices and experiences that characterized Kim's life. Respect for her memory is reflected in every word, every description that seeks to capture the authenticity of a person who lived with intensity and met difficulties with dignity. In this sense, the book aspires not only to be a faithful narrative but also to celebrate Kim Porter's courage and resilience.

An Invitation to Readers

This book is an invitation to truly know Kim Porter, beyond appearances and magazine covers, to discover the authentic woman, loving mother, and resilient individual who faced a life full of challenges with grace. It is a journey through her experiences, one that we hope conveys the depth of a complex and captivating personality—a figure who uniquely combined gentleness with inner strength. Through these pages, readers will encounter both her triumphs and the challenges that led her to grow and transform.

We invite every reader to connect with her story, to be touched by her choices, her feelings, and the bonds she built. Through these pages, we hope to convey the values and lessons Kim left, not only for her family and friends but for anyone who approaches life with the same desire for authenticity. Whether a longtime follower or someone learning about her for the first time, we hope that each reader finds inspiration and strength in Kim's journey.

Her story is more than a biography; it is a tale of resilience and hope, an example of how one can live with integrity and stay true to oneself even in difficult times. Kim Porter shows us that behind every success are unseen battles, that love for family can be a guiding light in dark moments, and that true beauty is found in inner strength. In a world that often judges by appearances, her life reminds us to seek deeper meaning, to value relationships, and to remember the importance of authenticity.

With this book, we wish for Kim's memory to live on and continue to inspire. Every word is written with respect and admiration for who she was, and each chapter is a homage to her legacy. We hope readers conclude this journey with a new understanding, not only of Kim Porter's life but also of what it means to live passionately, face adversity, and leave a legacy of love and light. Her story is a gift, and this book is an opportunity to explore it together.

Chapter 1: Roots in Columbus

A Southern City at Heart

Columbus, Georgia, is more than just a southern city in the United States; it is a place deeply rooted in tradition and family bonds, where community life plays a vital role in daily routines. Nestled along the banks of the Chattahoochee River, Columbus has evolved over time while retaining a strong connection to its cultural and social heritage. Growing up in this environment significantly shaped Kim Porter's character and worldview.

Known for its history and relaxed pace, Columbus offers a glimpse into Southern culture, where belonging and personal relationships are paramount. This environment allowed Kim to grow up where mutual support and traditional values were the cornerstones of life. The local community, filled with warmth and solidarity characteristic of Southern culture, played an essential role in her upbringing, teaching her the importance of caring for others and maintaining a deep connection to her roots.

In a place like Columbus, family is defined broadly to include not only close relatives but also friends and neighbors. Here, Kim learned to view the community as an extended family—a group ready to support each other during tough times and celebrate daily joys together. The experiences in her hometown instilled values that she would carry throughout her life, forging a resilient personality and a strong sense of adaptability.

This bond with Columbus was a source of stability and comfort for Kim, a safe harbor she could return to during uncertain times. The city, with its slower pace and closeness to nature, taught her to appreciate simple, genuine things, creating a solid foundation upon which to build her dreams and ambitions.

The Importance of Family and Community

Growing up in an environment like Columbus meant that Kim was immersed in authentic relationships where mutual support was a firm foundation. Her family life was her first reference point, a core that supported her and instilled essential values like generosity and respect. These principles extended beyond her home, into her neighborhood, which became an extension of familial warmth and a constant example of solidarity.

In this context, everyone contributed to maintaining a sense of belonging and stability that left a lasting impression on Kim. It was a place where people naturally took care of each other, where helping others came instinctively. From relatives to friends and even casual acquaintances, everyone represented a safety net and source of support—a community of faces and stories that influenced her growth and shaped her approach to others.

The guidance she received, based on real-life examples of love and responsibility, shaped her deep, genuine view of relationships. Kim learned to value kindness and resilience, understanding that success wasn't solely about personal achievements but about the ability to spread love and understanding. Even in life's most challenging moments, the principles she learned early on would serve as a moral compass.

These strong roots allowed her to approach the world with a well-defined identity. Even when her career took her far from home, the values she acquired in her youth remained the foundation upon which she built her life, influencing her decisions and becoming a legacy she would carry with her always.

Sarah Porter: A Model of Strength

Sarah Porter, Kim's mother, was a woman of extraordinary resilience, facing life's challenges with a grace and strength that inspired her daughter. Having grown up in an environment that taught her to overcome daily hardships, Sarah was a model of determination for Kim, a guiding light in uncertain times. With a natural pragmatism and unconditional love for her family, Sarah taught Kim that true strength lies in staying calm in the face of adversity.

One story Kim often recalled was a moment from her childhood when she struggled with schoolwork. Sarah would sit by her side, guiding her with patience and encouraging her not to get discouraged. "You don't have to be perfect," she would say, "just do your best, because that's what really matters." This lesson would accompany Kim throughout her life, reminding her that perfection wasn't necessary for success—that dedication and consistency were the true keys to achieving one's goals.

Sarah was also intent on teaching Kim the importance of empathy and kindness. She often took time to visit neighbors and friends in need, bringing Kim along to teach her the value of helping others. During these visits, she would explain to Kim that being strong didn't mean being hard; it meant being present for others, even in difficult moments. This lesson stayed with Kim, shaping many of her choices as an adult, where respect for others and the ability to care for those close to her became integral parts of her character.

Despite the financial and social challenges they sometimes faced, Sarah approached every situation with dignity. Even in unfavorable circumstances, she worked to instill confidence in Kim, reminding her that their worth wasn't defined by what they owned but by who they were. Her mother often told her,

"What really matters isn't how others see us but how we see ourselves." This phrase became a sort of mantra for Kim, an encouragement to build her own identity and stay true to her values.

The bond between mother and daughter wasn't just affectionate; it was an alliance based on mutual respect. Sarah was much more than a guide for Kim; she was a living example of how self-respect and determination could transform even the toughest challenges into opportunities for growth. She was a woman who, though without great means, could infuse those around her with a sense of peace and inner strength.

Every night, Sarah spoke to Kim about her dreams and the potential she saw in her, inspiring her to believe in herself. It was clear that Sarah wanted a life for her daughter beyond the limits of their neighborhood, filled with opportunities. This bond, built on trust and mutual respect, would stay with Kim throughout her life, allowing her to face the future with a heart full of love and lasting lessons.

Joys and Challenges of Childhood

Kim's childhood, spent along the familiar streets of Columbus, was a mix of joyful moments and small challenges that helped forge her strong character. From an early age, she learned to appreciate the little joys of everyday life: laughter shared with neighborhood friends, evenings listening to stories from adults, and days spent outdoors exploring every corner of her world. These were simple yet meaningful moments that taught her to find beauty even in the ordinary.

At the same time, she faced difficulties that prepared her for bigger challenges ahead. In a community like hers, it wasn't always easy to aspire to dreams beyond the city's boundaries. However, even at a young age, she displayed a natural determination that pushed her to look beyond and never settle.

Confronting these small trials taught her the value of patience and perseverance—qualities she would carry with her for the rest of her life.

A significant episode reflecting her resilient spirit involved her early attempts to excel in school. Despite the challenges, with the support of her mother and community, she learned to view each obstacle as a chance for growth. Thanks to this supportive environment, she developed a calm approach to challenges and the awareness that every step forward was a milestone toward something greater.

Her childhood thus represented a crucial phase of learning and building, where she accumulated experiences that would guide her future steps. Through the joys and challenges of those days, she developed a positive outlook and an inner strength that would prove invaluable throughout her life.

Moments of Carefree Joy and Childhood Dreams

Kim's childhood was also a time of exploration, imagination, and shared dreams. The years spent in Columbus were filled with carefree moments: racing with friends along neighborhood streets, playing in fields, and the infectious laughter filling summer evenings. Every corner of the city became a magical place for new adventures, and each friendship an opportunity to see the world through the innocent eyes of childhood.

In those days, Kim's dreams expanded beyond the boundaries of her hometown. Between games, she often spoke with friends about what it would be like to explore new places and live in big cities. She was drawn to the idea of discovering new places, meeting different people, and building a life that reached beyond what she knew. These early desires, though still innocent, already signaled the ambition that would later find expression.

These moments of play and imagination weren't just pastimes but a safe space where Kim could dream freely and imagine a future filled with possibilities. Her friends' conversations spanned a variety of ideas: some dreamed of adventurous lives, others of becoming artists, and others still of traveling. For her, each dream was a small window to the world, an invitation never to limit herself to what was right in front of her.

These years of youth allowed her to develop an insatiable curiosity for life and a desire for exploration that would become the driving force behind her future projects. She knew her dreams might seem grand, but her mother's and friends' support gave her the confidence to believe in them. The imagined adventures lived in the streets of Columbus were the prelude to a real journey that would lead her to experience worlds and people beyond her wildest expectations.

A Mother's Support in the Early Years

During her formative years, her mother's support was an invaluable resource that encouraged Kim to explore her dreams and believe in her abilities. Sarah was not only a guide but also a constant source of encouragement and inspiration, always ready to push her daughter to look beyond apparent limits and chase her ambitions.

From an early age, Sarah recognized the unique spark in Kim—a rare curiosity and determination. When her daughter shared her aspirations, her mother listened attentively, conveying the message that every dream, no matter how big, was worth nurturing. It wasn't just words of encouragement; Sarah helped Kim understand that with dedication and effort, nothing was out of reach. This support would accompany her throughout her life, bolstering her confidence in transforming dreams into reality.

Sarah encouraged her daughter to express herself and pursue her interests, always balancing dreams with reality. She urged her to put effort into everything, reminding her that the path to success is paved with small steps and thoughtful choices. "You can become whatever you want," she often said, "but you have to be willing to work hard." This advice would stay with Kim in the years to come, fueling her entrepreneurial spirit and her ability to face challenges with determination.

Sarah's support went beyond encouragement; she was present in every part of Kim's life, helping her build a positive self-view and sense of her possibilities. Every time her daughter faced a difficulty or felt uncertain, her mother was there to support her, offering practical advice and hope. Sarah didn't want her child to grow up with mental or emotional limitations; she wanted her to be aware of her potential and face life with an open and courageous spirit.

This bond of support, trust, and understanding formed a solid foundation, allowing Kim to take her first steps toward a future she no longer feared to imagine. Sarah's teachings would continue to inspire her throughout her life, reminding her that even in tough times, the love and support of family are an unstoppable force.

Values of Resilience and Determination

From a young age, Kim absorbed values that would become central to her character and life choices. In a setting that often presented challenges, she developed a resilience that allowed her to adapt to any situation and a determination that kept her moving forward. Life in the South, with its traditions and steady rhythm, taught her that courage wasn't about avoiding difficulties but about meeting them with constant inner strength.

Kim observed her mother and the adults around her, learning from them the art of standing firm even when life seemed challenging. The perseverance of Sarah and those close to her gave her a valuable lesson: no matter how big the obstacles might seem, the key is to stay calm and move forward with integrity and confidence. From these experiences, young Kim understood that, despite circumstances, she had the power to shape her destiny through conscious and consistent choices.

Over the years, these values became an inseparable part of who she was. Whenever she faced uncertainty or personal challenges, Kim recalled the teachings she had received, remembering the importance of believing in herself and not being swayed by others' opinions or judgments. This conviction allowed her to face the future with a confidence that came not from external circumstances but from a strength built over time, day by day.

For her, resilience wasn't merely passive endurance but a continual process of growth. Even when things seemed complicated, she always found a way to get back up, learn, and move forward with renewed awareness. This way of life represented Kim's true strength, an adaptability that would support her through all the challenges of her career and personal life.

A Solid Foundation for the Future

Columbus wasn't just the city where Kim grew up; it was the place that gave her a solid foundation for her future. In those familiar streets and among the people who watched her grow, she developed the values and skills that would guide her decisions for a lifetime. Every lesson learned, from the small challenges faced with her mother's support to her determination in following her dreams, became an essential part of the resilience that would become her defining trait.

As she grew, Kim understood that the world beyond Columbus held new opportunities, but that her roots and lessons learned would always be with her. Her hometown had instilled in her an inner balance and the ability to face difficulties with a steady spirit—values that enabled her to look to the future without forgetting her origins. Knowing she had a secure base behind her gave her the courage to look beyond, imagining a life where she could fulfill her potential.

The decision to leave Columbus for Atlanta represented an important and challenging step. On one hand, she had a desire to explore new horizons and make a name for herself in a larger world; on the other, she was certain that, no matter what happened, she could always rely on the values and teachings she had received. This solid foundation allowed her to face the uncertainties of the future with confidence, knowing that the deep roots she had developed in her childhood were the true pillars of her identity.

Chapter 2: Early Dreams and Moving to Atlanta

The Ambition to Move Beyond Columbus

As she grew, Kim felt an increasing desire to broaden her horizons, to explore new paths and discover what the world had to offer beyond the boundaries of her hometown. While Columbus had given her all the support she needed, there was a natural drive within her to look beyond, to imagine a life where she could fulfill her greatest ambitions. This desire to move beyond wasn't merely a quest for success; it was a hunger to grow, to challenge herself, and to test her capabilities.

Whenever she heard about big cities like Atlanta, Kim envisioned herself surrounded by possibilities—a place where her potential could fully shine. She knew this step would be challenging and require sacrifices, but her determination to follow her dreams was stronger than any doubt. Her roots had given her the confidence to face even the biggest changes, enabling her to look to the future with enthusiasm.

Her ambition to break free from the limitations of her original environment was an unstoppable energy, a drive that pushed her to seek opportunities where she could express her talents. The idea of leaving and building something new for herself wasn't just a dream; it was a life plan. Kim knew that her ambitions would lead her far and that each step toward the future was a step closer to realizing the potential she had felt within herself since childhood.

First Experiences in Fashion

As her dream of leaving Columbus grew, Kim found in her early experiences in fashion a tangible way to inch closer to the world she so deeply wished to explore. Fashion wasn't just a professional opportunity; it was a form of self-expression that allowed her to convey who she was and who she aspired to become. Through her style and presence, she could show the world her unique blend of elegance, charisma, and determination.

Her first fashion shows and photo shoots weren't the grand events of international runways, but for Kim, they were experiences filled with excitement and confidence. Each small opportunity confirmed that her bold dream, audacious for a girl from Columbus, could indeed become a reality. These local events, though modest, served as a launching pad—an opportunity to hone her skills and learn how to navigate an industry that demanded strength and confidence.

During these early experiences, Kim met others who, like her, were drawn to the world of fashion and shared her passion for art and creativity. These encounters allowed her to expand her network and connect with those who understood the industry, giving her a taste of what it meant to work in this field. Working with photographers, stylists, and other models, she learned the challenges and difficulties that defined the fashion world, along with the satisfaction that came from seeing her efforts take shape.

Each experience allowed her to grow and mature, fueling her desire to reach for ever-greater achievements. These early trials helped her build a confidence that would prepare her for her leap to Atlanta, where she would face a larger audience and even more exciting challenges. Aware that the road would be long, the trust she built step by step gave her the strength to look toward the future with optimism and determination.

Atlanta: The Gateway to a New World

After her first experiences in Columbus, Kim felt the need to expand her horizons and immerse herself in an environment that could offer new opportunities and greater visibility. Moving to Atlanta was a crucial step—a turning point for her career and personal growth. Known for its rapidly evolving arts and cultural scene, Atlanta was the perfect place for an aspiring model eager to make her mark. The city promised not only more career possibilities but also a more stimulating and dynamic environment compared to her hometown.

Right after high school, Kim moved to Atlanta, full of expectations and a desire to test herself in a larger world. The city offered an ideal context for nurturing her ambitions: local modeling agencies, numerous events, and fashion shows allowed her to refine her skills and gain visibility. Thanks to her natural talent and determination, Kim began building a network of professional contacts, paving the way for increasingly significant opportunities.

However, Atlanta wasn't just a city full of possibilities; it was a proving ground that demanded resilience and motivation. Far from the security and support of her original community, she faced the challenges of a new city and a highly competitive environment. Yet, her inner strength and the lessons she learned in Columbus sustained her, allowing her to confront every obstacle with determination. She knew that each challenge overcome was another step toward success.

In short, moving to Atlanta not only broadened Kim's professional horizons but also offered her the chance to grow and establish herself in an environment that required dedication and adaptability. This move opened the door to a new world, laying the foundation for a career that would soon find its natural course, helping her emerge as a prominent figure in fashion and entertainment.

A Competitive Environment and New Challenges

Arriving in Atlanta marked a true shift in perspective for Kim. Used to the familiarity and support of her Columbus community, she now found herself in a dynamic, highly competitive city where standing out required commitment and adaptability. Each day presented an opportunity, but also a challenge: the fashion world in Atlanta demanded determination and a desire to distinguish oneself in an environment filled with talent and opportunities reserved only for those who proved themselves persistent and bold.

Kim quickly realized that making a career here would mean overcoming various obstacles. Away from the support network she had always relied on, she learned to depend on herself and find motivation within. Local fashion shows and photo shoots offered her limited visibility but were precious opportunities to refine her skills and make herself noticed. Every small success affirmed her potential and encouraged her to push past her limits.

In this new environment, Kim developed an even stronger resilience, shaped by the difficulties she faced and the lessons learned along the way. Every rejection and missed opportunity became formative experiences that prepared her for future challenges. She understood that talent alone wasn't enough; building a network, demonstrating professionalism, and confidently presenting herself were all essential.

Kim's determination and ability to face difficulties with a positive attitude helped her overcome moments of discouragement. Atlanta gave her a taste of what it meant to work seriously in fashion, teaching her that success never comes without effort and sacrifice. This experience helped her build a mindset focused on growth—a resource that would prove invaluable for the challenges ahead.

Moments of Solitude and Her Mother's Support

Despite the enthusiasm and determination that characterized her move to Atlanta, Kim found herself dealing with a sense of loneliness she hadn't anticipated. Far from the city she grew up in and the support of the Columbus community, she often felt the absence of the familiarity that had always been a part of her life. Each new challenge, every moment of uncertainty, amplified that distance from her roots, forcing her to confront a reality that, though exciting, was at times foreign and isolating.

In those moments of solitude, her bond with her mother became crucial. Sarah, who had always encouraged her to follow her dreams, remained a constant presence, even from afar. Phone calls with her mother were a comforting anchor, offering her a sense of belonging and stability. Sarah didn't just provide words of encouragement; she reminded Kim of the values and principles she had grown up with, inspiring her to stay true to herself even in a competitive environment.

Her mother's emotional support was not only a source of comfort but also a guide that helped her manage the stress and challenges of life in a new city. Sarah conveyed the message that, even in the toughest moments, it was important to remain true to oneself and not lose sight of one's worth. Whenever Kim felt overwhelmed, she found the strength to rise again and face Atlanta's challenges through her connection with her mother.

This period of adaptation, though difficult, allowed Kim to strengthen her character and recognize the importance of family support. The distance from Columbus and the confrontation with a new world helped her mature and develop an even deeper awareness of her abilities. Even in moments of loneliness, she knew she wasn't truly alone, and this awareness gave her the strength to move forward confidently.

Initial Contacts and Opportunities in Atlanta's Fashion Scene

Moving to Atlanta not only opened new doors for Kim but also allowed her to connect with influential people in the fashion industry. In this dynamic city, each event was an opportunity to expand her network and forge connections that could turn her aspirations into reality. The fashion shows and photo shoots she participated in gradually gained importance, and Kim began to make a name for herself with her determination and stage presence that captured attention.

Thanks to her natural talent and adaptability, she succeeded in forming professional relationships with photographers, stylists, and other models, laying the foundation for a career in an industry where personal connections were crucial. Each new encounter provided her with not only valuable experiences but also the chance to learn from the people she collaborated with. Kim understood the importance of these contacts and worked hard to build solid relationships based on trust and mutual respect—essential elements for carving out a space in such a competitive field.

Significant opportunities weren't long in coming. Participating in more prominent events and collaborating with established professionals gave her an additional boost, increasing her visibility and strengthening her reputation as a serious and talented model. These small achievements reminded her that every sacrifice made so far was worth it, motivating her to continue working with passion and commitment.

Before long, Atlanta became more than just a city of opportunities; it was a stepping stone toward an even more ambitious future. Every contact and collaboration brought her one step closer to her goals, turning her aspirations into a concrete, achievable project.

Reaching Small Milestones and Fueling the Dream

In Atlanta, every small milestone reached represented a confirmation of her path. Each successful fashion show and photo shoot reminded Kim that her dedication and passion were building something solid. Far from the simplicity of Columbus, Kim felt that every step forward was an achievement that brought her closer to her goals.

These small successes, though they may have seemed minor, were actually essential steps that fueled her motivation. Every completed assignment or positive feedback made her dream of a fashion career feel more tangible. These moments of personal and professional growth helped strengthen her self-esteem, reminding her that she was on the right path and that, with determination and persistence, she could achieve much more.

Kim understood that the road to success wouldn't be linear and that the true value lay in continuing to put in the effort, no matter the size of the outcome. She fed her dream with every small milestone, letting the confidence she accumulated over time propel her to face future challenges with even more enthusiasm and ambition. Thanks to these successes, Kim built a solid professional identity—a foundation upon which she could grow a career destined to flourish.

A Clearer Vision of the Future

As her career in Atlanta became more established, Kim developed an increasingly clear vision of what she wanted for her future. Her early experiences in the fashion world, though limited, had given her a taste of what it could mean to live a life filled with fulfilled ambitions. With each new contact and opportunity, Kim began to outline a path that extended beyond local fashion, envisioning horizons that only a city like Atlanta could inspire.

This vision of a future in fashion was fueled not only by determination but by a passion that grew with every new challenge faced and overcome. Over time, Kim no longer merely dreamed; she began actively planning the next steps in her career. She knew that while her experience so far was valuable, reaching higher levels would require continuous evolution and refinement. The idea of leaving her mark on the industry became increasingly concrete, transforming into a goal she was determined to pursue.

This vision kept her focused, even in the most challenging moments, reminding her why she had chosen such a demanding path. Kim learned that patience and confidence in her potential were essential qualities for realizing her dreams— qualities that would be invaluable in the next stages of her life. The knowledge that each sacrifice and success was a fundamental piece of her journey filled her with an unwavering determination.

At this point, Kim no longer saw success as a simple destination but as an ongoing journey—a series of experiences that would enrich her and strengthen her confidence in her abilities. Thanks to this clear vision and the tenacity she had built over time, she was ready to take the next step, one that would bring her even closer to the heart of the fashion world and to achieving her most ambitious goals.

Chapter 3: New Experiences in the Fashion World

The First Meeting with a Modeling Agency

Kim's first meeting with a modeling agency in Atlanta marked the beginning of a new chapter. With her heart racing, she stepped into the elegant office, fully aware of the importance of making a good impression. She had prepared carefully, considering every detail from her outfit to her posture, working to overcome the insecurities that often emerge in unfamiliar situations. The waiting room, with its decorated walls and bright lights, only amplified the tension. Yet, under that pressure, Kim found the strength to stay calm and project confidence.

When she was finally called in, her adrenaline surged. The agency representatives greeted her with attentive gazes, evaluating her every move. Kim knew her appearance alone wouldn't be enough—she had to demonstrate character, presence, and a determination that went beyond surface beauty. With a steady voice and a focused look, she introduced herself, sharing her background and her aspiration to build a career in fashion.

After the meeting, she felt a mix of anxiety and hope, but the pride of having faced such a challenge filled her with confidence. She had taken an important first step, proving to herself that she could handle even the most demanding situations.

First Photoshoots: A Transformative Experience

When it came time for her first photoshoots, Kim felt a blend of excitement and uncertainty. Standing before the camera for the first time, she felt as if she were under a magnifying glass, with every nuance of her face and expression amplified and captured. As the photographer prepared, Kim tried to mask her anxiety, knowing these images would represent her first tangible steps into the fashion world.

Initially, her poses were stiff, and she felt vulnerable in front of the camera. However, observing the professionals around her, she learned to relax and to embrace her role with more awareness. Each shot became an opportunity to express a part of herself, to let her personality shine through the lens. Gradually, she began to understand the importance of light, angles, and details—elements that helped highlight her image and build her unique style.

These first photoshoots became a training ground where Kim honed her skills and discovered new facets of herself. Each session helped her grow, building her confidence and transforming her initial insecurity into an authentic, magnetic presence. The guidance of experienced photographers, who offered valuable advice, helped her develop a new self-assurance and a strength that would serve her well throughout her fashion journey.

A World of Appearances and Reality

In the world of fashion, Kim quickly learned that appearances were only part of the reality. Behind the elegance of photoshoots and runways lay a competitive environment where every detail was meticulously controlled, and every mistake could be magnified. Kim's first impression was of a fascinating yet complex world, where beauty and perfection were often the result of hours of preparation and painstaking work.

Despite her initial excitement, Kim had to adapt to an environment with high expectations and constant pressure. Image was everything, and the professionals around her made it clear that she would need to demonstrate discipline and determination to stand out. Each photoshoot and runway show represented an opportunity but also a test of endurance, where she had to prove her worth among many other talented and ambitious individuals.

This at times harsh reality allowed Kim to see beyond appearances and understand the importance of maintaining a strong personal identity. The fashion world could be ruthless, but every experience taught her something new, helping her grow and develop a deeper awareness of her strengths. Over time, she learned to balance external expectations with her desire for authenticity, transforming each challenge into an opportunity to affirm herself.

The Challenge of Staying Authentic

Immersed in the fashion world, Kim soon realized how difficult it was to keep her authenticity intact. In an environment where image and appearance meant everything, resisting external pressures required inner strength and self-awareness that few could maintain. The constant pursuit of perfection and the ongoing comparison to beauty standards imposed by the industry could easily lead anyone to lose sight of their true self.

However, Kim understood that her strength lay not just in her appearance but in her ability to remain true to herself. Each time she felt the pressure to conform, she found a balance between industry demands and the values with which she was raised. She often remembered her mother's advice, which had always emphasized the importance of being honest with herself and respecting her identity, regardless of the circumstances.

This commitment to authenticity became a core value and a guiding principle in a journey that could have otherwise led her to lose her individuality. Kim realized that true success wasn't measured by fame or the number of jobs secured, but by the ability to look in the mirror and recognize herself. This lesson allowed her to stand out in the industry, not just for her talent but for her integrity.

A Photographer Friend and Valuable Advice

During one of her first photoshoots in Atlanta, Kim met an experienced photographer who would play an important role in her personal and professional growth. A special bond quickly formed between them, built on mutual respect and the photographer's willingness to guide her through the complexities of the fashion industry. This friendship became a source of valuable advice and support, offering Kim essential tools to improve her skills.

The photographer didn't just teach her techniques and poses; he encouraged her to express herself, to find the naturalness that would make her unique in front of the camera. Kim learned that each pose shouldn't just be an aesthetic position but a way to communicate her true essence. With patience, her friend taught her to transform insecurity into confidence, to look at the lens with assurance and convey authenticity in every shot.

Thanks to his guidance, Kim developed greater self-awareness and a deeper connection with photography. His advice to always be sincere in her expressions and to maintain her style, even under pressure, helped her build a solid foundation for the future. This support allowed her to refine her talent and stand out in a field where inner truth is often sacrificed for appearance. Her experience with this photographer became a life lesson, teaching her that authentic beauty comes from confidence and self-acceptance.

The First Major Runway Show: Kim's Heartbeat

Her first major runway show was a pivotal moment in Kim's fashion journey. The event took place at one of Atlanta's prime venues, attracting the attention of industry professionals and fashion enthusiasts alike. Behind the scenes, the atmosphere was charged with energy and tension; models, designers, and makeup artists worked frantically to ensure the show's success.

Waiting for her turn, Kim felt her heart beating fast. She wore an elegant dress, the work of an emerging designer, and knew that each step on the runway would be closely watched. As she prepared, she thought about the advice she had received from her photographer friend and her mother's encouraging words, which had always reminded her of the importance of staying true to herself.

When her moment finally came, Kim took a deep breath and walked out with confidence. The intense lights and the audience's gaze could have been intimidating, but she transformed that pressure into determination. Each step was measured, each look intentional; she felt that she belonged in that world and that she had found her place.

At the end of the show, the applause from the audience and the compliments from her colleagues confirmed she was on the right path. That experience not only reinforced her confidence but also gave her a clearer vision of the future she wanted to build in the fashion industry.

Criticism and Life Lessons

Along her journey, Kim quickly learned that the fashion world, though glamorous, wasn't without criticism. The sharp eyes of professionals, the comments from colleagues, and even public opinion often scrutinized every aspect of her work. Sometimes, these judgments were harsh, affecting her self-esteem and making her question her abilities. However, instead of letting herself be discouraged, Kim found in these experiences an opportunity for growth and reflection.

Whenever she received criticism, she recalled her mother's teachings, which emphasized the importance of maintaining her integrity. Sarah had encouraged her to view each challenge as a learning opportunity and to consider others' opinions as tools for improvement without losing sight of her values. This approach helped her turn each comment, even the toughest ones, into a life lesson.

Over time, Kim learned to filter criticism, distinguishing between constructive feedback and comments meant only to demoralize her. She realized that, to succeed, she had to continue believing in herself and her journey. The challenges she encountered only strengthened her character, allowing her to develop resilience and confidence that would stay with her for life.

This experience taught her to welcome feedback as a valuable resource, learning to use it to grow both professionally and personally. Criticism thus became an integral part of her journey, shaping a stronger and more mature view of herself and her worth.

A First Glimpse at the Big City: New York on the Horizon

With each experience in Atlanta, Kim felt an increasing desire to explore even broader horizons. The city had offered her countless opportunities for professional growth, but she knew that to reach the beating heart of fashion, she would have to take an even bigger step. The ideal destination to bring her dreams to life was New York City.

The thought of moving to such a dynamic, opportunity-rich environment filled her with excitement, even though she knew she would face significant challenges. Away from the security of Atlanta, she would have to prove herself in an even more competitive and selective arena. Yet, the allure of that metropolis and her ambition to succeed fueled her determination.

In the months leading up to her departure, she prepared thoroughly, researching top agencies, making connections, and studying the industry. Every lesson learned from criticism and every small milestone achieved until that point motivated her to face this new challenge with courage. Her preparation was meticulous, and deep down, she knew this change would be crucial.

Ready to take the leap, she approached the next chapter of her life with confidence. The city of her dreams awaited, and Kim felt ready to leave her mark, carrying with her all the lessons gathered along the way.

Chapter 4: Moving to New York: A New Beginning

The Courage to Leave Atlanta

Leaving Atlanta was not an easy choice for Kim. She had built a network, gained confidence, and achieved her first milestones, but she felt that to truly grow, she would have to push herself further. The prospect of moving to New York filled her with excitement but also with a fair amount of apprehension. Atlanta had given her stability and helped her define her style and character. Now, leaving it all behind to enter an even more competitive world required extraordinary courage.

In the days leading up to her departure, Kim reflected on what she had accomplished and what awaited her in the big city. New York was a challenge—a place where every step would be observed and judged. However, she felt that her inner strength and the support of those she loved would give her the push she needed to overcome any difficulty. She knew New York wouldn't grant any favors, but the idea of discovering her full potential in such a stimulating environment filled her with determination.

With a mixture of excitement and nostalgia, Kim said goodbye to Atlanta, carrying with her the lessons and memories of her experiences. The journey to New York was more than a physical move; it was a symbolic step toward a future where she would test herself like never before. With her heart full of dreams and hopes, she was ready to take on the city she had long envisioned as the perfect stage for achieving her goals.

Life in a New City: The Impact of New York

Arriving in New York was an overwhelming dive into a fast-paced, complex reality. The city, with its relentless rhythm and multitude of unfamiliar faces, struck her immediately, making her feel the weight of a challenge that was very different from the one she had faced in Atlanta. Each day, the streets teemed with activity, and every corner seemed to offer both opportunities and obstacles, woven together in an endless array of possibilities.

The first few weeks were marked by a sense of disorientation. Adjusting to such a vast environment wasn't easy—every part of her life seemed to demand adaptation and sacrifice. Yet, thanks to her resilience, she gradually began to see the city as a growth opportunity. With the same determination that had guided her thus far, she worked to find a balance between the excitement and the pressure that this new world entailed.

Over time, she learned to navigate the city's unyielding pace and to recognize the hidden opportunities within its challenges. This period of adjustment became an essential phase, a proving ground that allowed her to strengthen her character. The city not only offered her work opportunities but pushed her to evolve, helping her surpass limits that once seemed insurmountable, preparing her for all that the future held.

New Contacts and the Fashion Network

One of the first lessons Kim learned in New York was the importance of connections. In a city where everyone seemed to be racing toward their goals, professional relationships weren't just opportunities; they were essential bridges to new achievements. Aware of this, she started attending exclusive events, parties, and fashion shows—occasions where the doors of that still somewhat inaccessible world seemed to open.

One evening, at a fashion event in Soho, Kim had the chance to meet a well-known agent who represented some of the top models in the industry. The encounter happened entirely by chance; as she watched a show, she exchanged a few words with him about the collection on display. That brief conversation, born from a simple interest in fashion, turned into a deeper exchange, where she conveyed her passion and determination. This connection proved crucial, as the agent opened doors to new opportunities and collaborations that had previously been out of her reach.

Every new acquaintance was not only a professional opportunity but also a way for her to better understand the dynamics of this competitive yet stimulating world. Kim quickly learned to present herself with confidence, sharing her story and goals authentically, attracting the attention of those who could recognize talent and commitment. Each meeting contributed to shaping her path and provided her with the motivation to continue building her name in a world where image and reputation were everything.

The First Significant Collaborations

After months of hard work and persistence, Kim began to see the fruits of her efforts in New York. Her determination and ability to build genuine relationships led her to collaborate with major brands in the fashion industry. One of her first significant opportunities was a campaign for Tommy Hilfiger, where her natural elegance and stage presence captured the attention of the public and industry professionals.

Later, she was selected for a series of photo shoots for Pantene, becoming one of the faces of the brand. These collaborations not only increased her visibility but also allowed her to refine her professional skills, working with internationally renowned photographers and stylists.

Every new job represented a step forward in her career, affirming that her choice to move to New York had been the right one. These experiences gave her opportunities for both professional and personal growth, solidifying her position in the fashion world and paving the way for future prestigious collaborations.

The Challenge of Staying Grounded in a Volatile World

Despite her initial successes, Kim quickly realized that the fashion world in New York was extremely unpredictable. Opportunities could arise unexpectedly but could disappear just as quickly. Periods of intense work were often followed by moments of uncertainty, when job offers dwindled, and competition grew fiercer.

In these times, her determination was put to the test. The pressure to maintain a constant presence in the industry, combined with the financial demands of life in the Big Apple, was a daily challenge. Kim had to develop an inner resilience, learning to manage her anxiety and stay focused on her goals even when circumstances seemed unfavorable.

To overcome these challenges, she dedicated herself to constantly improving her skills, attending workshops, and working with different professionals to expand her portfolio. This proactive approach allowed her to stay relevant in an ever-evolving environment and to turn challenges into opportunities for personal and professional growth.

A New Friendship in the Industry

Through her work experiences, Kim met an emerging model who, like her, was trying to build a career in a competitive and often unforgiving industry. They immediately developed a special connection, based on a mutual understanding of the difficulties and challenges of the sector. Having someone by her side who knew the pressures, sacrifices, and moments of doubt became a precious support for Kim.

The two young models shared confidences, experiences, and advice, forming an alliance that helped them maintain balance. In a world where image was everything, this friendship offered them a refuge where they could be authentic without always needing to appear perfect. In the most challenging moments, such as when work was scarce or criticism was particularly harsh, Kim's friend served as a constant reminder to keep believing in herself.

This friendship not only provided the moral support she needed but also helped her develop a more balanced perspective on the fashion world, teaching her that true value lay beyond immediate success and could be found in the human connections made along the way.

Glimpses and Opportunities in Manhattan

As she became more immersed in the Manhattan scene, Kim began attending exclusive events and building connections that went beyond work. The city offered her a vibrant social life— a whirlwind of evenings, parties, and encounters that extended well beyond the fashion world. In these moments, surrounded by influential and charismatic people, Kim discovered new faces, new stories, and, at times, allowed herself to explore the possibility of finding a deeper connection.

In Manhattan, her elegance and natural charisma did not go unnoticed. Through these events, Kim began to see the possibility of creating something meaningful in her personal life as well, an aspiration that grew alongside her desire to establish a stability that extended beyond professional success. The chance encounters with fascinating, ambitious men sparked her curiosity to explore a new aspect of her life—the search for a partner with whom she could envision a future.

These exchanged glances and the conversations that unfolded during evenings in Manhattan offered her a glimpse of what the next chapter of her life could be. The city, with its lights and energy, was beginning to represent not only a place to grow her career but also a space where her heart could find new paths, ready to be explored.

A Decisive Step Toward Success

After months of sacrifice, commitment, and moments of uncertainty, Kim landed a job that would change the trajectory of her career. She was selected for a major advertising campaign—an opportunity that represented much more than just a job; it was confirmation that her talent and dedication had not gone unnoticed. In that moment, she understood that her decision to move to New York, with all its challenges, had been the right one.

The campaign cast her as the star, and working with a team of top professionals gave her the motivation to continue believing in her path. Each shot, each interaction with the team members, confirmed that she was exactly where she was meant to be. Kim felt she had found her voice and a professional identity that truly reflected who she was.

This experience not only solidified her position in the industry but also offered her a new perspective on her future. From that moment on, New York was no longer just a challenge but the place where she could genuinely fulfill her dreams. With the confidence of someone who has overcome difficult trials and a desire to look ahead, she was preparing for a future where professional success could intertwine with new personal discoveries and, perhaps, with the love she was beginning to seek.

Chapter 5: Meeting Al B. Sure! and the Birth of Quincy

A Life-Changing Encounter

It was an evening like any other in New York, yet for Kim, it would mark the beginning of something extraordinary. The city buzzed with lights and energy, and that particular social event, filled with music and laughter, was a swirl of familiar faces and fleeting glances. Amidst the crowd, Kim, still a relatively new face to many, felt swept up in the elegance and rhythm of the night. But as she scanned the room, her gaze settled on one particular figure.

Al B. Sure! was a prominent name in music, a producer and singer known not only for his success but also for his magnetic presence. Standing at the center of the room, he commanded attention effortlessly, as though everyone else naturally gravitated around him. Their eyes met, and in that instant, the atmosphere shifted. Kim felt captivated, as though the rest of the room had faded, leaving only a suspended moment between them.

Al approached Kim with a confident yet gentle smile, breaking the ice with a few words. They spoke like old friends reconnecting, sharing thoughts about the city, music, and dreams. His way of conversing—deep and sincere— immediately struck Kim, revealing to her something more than a celebrity. The chemistry between them was unexpected yet powerful, a connection that seemed to bypass the formalities of a social event and touch on their deepest aspirations.

That evening, Kim realized that this meeting would leave a lasting mark on her life. Al, with his experience and passion, appeared not only as a captivating figure but as a guide. His presence represented a new chapter, an opportunity to explore parts of herself she had yet to discover. In him, Kim found someone who could inspire her and, at the same time, offer a broader view of the possibilities that the future might hold.

The evening ended, but Al's impression lingered. Kim knew that the spark they felt was not one that would easily fade. That night, beneath the skyscrapers of New York, the beginning of a story was unfolding, one that would change not only her career but her heart.

An Intense and Passionate Relationship

In the weeks that followed, what had started as a chance encounter quickly transformed into a deep, all-encompassing bond. Kim and Al saw each other more frequently, carving out private moments away from the spotlight. Each encounter between them reignited a spark, fueling a passion that grew stronger by the day. Their relationship held a unique intensity, as though the outside world, with all its expectations and pressures, disappeared whenever they were together. Al became much more than just a partner for Kim; he was a confidant, a mentor—someone who could listen and understand her dreams without need for explanation.

With his experience in the music and entertainment world, Al possessed a charm and confidence that fascinated her. Beside him, Kim found both comfort and inspiration. Every time they spoke about their dreams, he encouraged her to believe in herself, to push beyond limits, and to persevere in the face of challenges. Al offered her valuable insights, sharing with her the secrets and struggles of a world he knew intimately. During those moments, Kim felt she could explore new dimensions of her personality, able to be authentic and vulnerable without fear of judgment.

Their love story was filled with intensity and passion but also with a sense of companionship. They cherished quiet evenings away from the city's glamour, engaging in intimate and sincere conversations. Those moments became a refuge for them both, a chance to truly get to know one another without the burden of social expectations. Kim valued Al's spontaneity, his ability to be present and appreciate her as a woman and as an individual. Beside him, she felt complete, as though she had found a missing piece of her life.

Their relationship, however, came with the weight of visibility. Being a high-profile couple was not easy; every public appearance drew the attention of the media and fans. Despite this, Kim and Al made an effort to keep their private lives as untouched as possible, protecting the precious bond they had built. Together, they found strength in each other, creating a relationship that, despite the challenges of fame, would last and profoundly impact both their lives.

Al's Influence on Her Life and Career

Al's influence on Kim's life extended far beyond romance; his experience and perspective on the entertainment world opened doors for Kim that had once seemed distant. With a successful music career behind him, Al knew the ins and outs of an industry where image, connections, and determination were paramount. Thanks to him, Kim was able to meet artists, producers, and influential figures she had only admired from afar. Every event Al brought her to became an opportunity for growth and discovery, a chance to broaden her horizons and better understand the challenges and opportunities in that complex world.

Always attentive and supportive, Al encouraged her to explore her potential. Each piece of advice was an invitation to not let obstacles hold her back, to view each hurdle as a stepping stone toward her goals. Al taught her to handle criticism with maturity, showing her that in show business, others' opinions could be either a hindrance or an opportunity for growth. Kim saw in him a patient guide and unwavering support, someone who deeply believed in her abilities and wanted her to realize her dreams of success.

These lessons, combined with the practical experience she was accumulating, helped Kim build new self-assurance. Thanks to Al, she began to see the entertainment world as an arena where a clear vision was essential, without ever sacrificing her authenticity. Under his guidance, Kim learned to navigate with greater awareness, to make thoughtful choices, and to protect her own value and image.

Their relationship became a bond rooted not only in love but in mutual growth. Al wanted Kim to find her voice, to express her talent without compromise. His influence offered her a new perspective, helping her understand that success was not solely about visibility but about building a solid career grounded in determination and authenticity. With Al by her side, Kim felt she could face any challenge with newfound strength, more self-aware and open to the possibilities life had to offer.

A Private Life in the Spotlight

As their relationship evolved, Kim and Al became an increasingly visible couple, drawing the attention of media and fans alike. Their love story, full of passion and companionship, was followed closely by the public, who saw in them a fascinating, talented couple. Yet, while they were both accustomed to the limelight, Kim and Al were determined to keep a part of their life private—a sanctuary away from the constant glare of attention.

Behind every public appearance, every pose, and every smile for the cameras was a desire to protect the authenticity of their relationship. Kim, aware of the pressures and expectations that came with success, worked to create a space just for them, a place where they were not two public figures but two people united by true love. Away from the cameras, they preferred quiet evenings in secluded places, sharing simple, genuine moments.

Together, they built a routine that helped them stay grounded. Kim and Al understood that to keep their relationship alive and strong, they needed to protect that intimate dimension, away from gossip and speculation. These moments of authenticity made them stronger, allowing them to live their relationship with a depth that the entertainment world rarely allows. Kim found comfort in these private moments, precious times where she could express every part of herself without worrying about maintaining a perfect image.

For Kim, defending that private side meant finding a balance between her public persona and her true self, between image and reality. With Al by her side, she discovered the value of discretion—the strength of a love that didn't need to be flaunted to be genuine. This understanding helped her better manage the pressures of visibility, showing her that while the public played an important role, their love and shared life belonged solely to them.

Kim's Desire to Build a Family

As her relationship with Al deepened, a long-held desire emerged within Kim—the wish to start a family. With Al, she felt that the time had finally come to turn that dream into reality. The love they shared was intense and genuine, making her feel ready to embark on a shared and lasting life journey. With him, Kim saw the possibility of creating a stable bond and beginning a new adventure that would deepen the scope of their relationship.

Since she was young, Kim had dreamed of becoming a mother, inspired by the teachings of her own mother, Sarah, who had always shown her the preciousness of family bonds. Sarah had instilled in Kim values of care, protection, and unconditional love—qualities Kim now wished to pass on to her own children. With Al, that dream seemed within reach, and the thought of building a family with him filled her with a deep, quiet joy.

Together, Kim and Al began discussing their future, imagining what their life with a child would be like. They shared dreams, hopes, and aspirations, building a common vision day by day. Al, with his kindness and constant support, reassured Kim, making her desire for motherhood feel more than just a dream. She knew that with him, she would have the strength to face the joys and challenges that this role would bring.

For Kim, the idea of becoming a mother was not only a personal milestone but a journey that would strengthen her bond with Al. She felt that building a family together would bring a new dimension to their relationship, intertwining their love with an even deeper connection. This desire for motherhood, born from the security and affection she felt with him, represented a step toward a fulfilling life rooted in the values she believed in and the hope of a shared future.

The News of Pregnancy: A New Adventure

When Kim discovered she was expecting a child, it felt like a wave of pure joy washed over her. This new chapter in her life was the start of a unique adventure—a transformation she felt deeply and anticipated eagerly. Motherhood was more than a dream for her; it was a journey she had long desired, and now it seemed within reach.

During the early months of pregnancy, Kim began to feel a special connection with the little one growing inside her. Every moment, every new sensation made her increasingly aware of the importance of this role, of how much she wanted to give her best to welcome this new life. With Al's support, who shared her joy and excitement, she prepared to embrace motherhood with a dedication and commitment that made her stronger.

This period represented not only a new challenge but an opportunity for growth and to fully understand the value of unconditional love. Pregnancy, with its emotions and expectations, offered her the chance to discover parts of herself she had never explored, strengthening her appreciation and love for the life that was about to begin.

The Support of Her Mother and the Significance of This Phase

During her pregnancy, Kim's bond with her mother, Sarah, grew even deeper. The maternal figure who had raised her with love and dedication became a valuable guide, a constant presence offering wisdom and advice for this new stage of life. Sarah, who understood every facet of motherhood, dedicated herself to supporting Kim, instilling in her a sense of calm and confidence for the future that was unfolding.

Each conversation between them became a source of comfort and inspiration. Sarah passed down timeless lessons, gestures, and traditions that came from their family and that Kim now prepared to share with her own child. Kim absorbed every word, knowing that these shared moments would form the foundation of her own experience as a mother. Her relationship with Sarah provided her not only practical support but also a profound sense of meaning, reminding her of the importance of family love and the roots that had always guided her.

This support was an essential pillar for her, allowing her to face pregnancy with greater peace and confidence. Her mother's presence reminded her that motherhood was a journey of discovery, one that required patience and devotion, and that unconditional love was the foundation upon which everything was built. In these moments, Kim felt she had all she needed to embrace her new life with an open heart and a strong spirit.

The Arrival of Quincy: An Incomparable Joy

In December 1991, Kim and Al joyfully welcomed the birth of their first child, Quincy Taylor Brown. They named him Quincy in honor of the legendary music producer Quincy Jones, a close friend of Al B. Sure! Quincy's arrival marked a moment of indescribable happiness for Kim, who felt complete in her new role as a mother.

The first months of motherhood were a period of discovery and adjustment. Kim faced the daily challenges with dedication, learning to balance her own needs with those of her newborn. Each smile from Quincy, each small milestone, filled her heart with a deep joy, strengthening the bond between mother and son.

Al's presence during this period was invaluable. Despite his professional commitments, he made an effort to be present, offering support and sharing parental responsibilities. Their home became a haven of love and serenity, where the family could grow away from the spotlight.

Kim also found support from her mother, Sarah, who offered invaluable advice and guided her through her new responsibilities. This strengthened family bond provided Kim with the strength to face the challenges of motherhood.

Quincy's arrival brought new perspective to Kim's life. Her priorities shifted, and the desire to provide her son with a safe and loving environment became central. This period marked the beginning of a phase of personal growth in which Kim learned to balance the demands of her career with those of her family, building a life filled with purpose and love.

The Early Months of Motherhood: Challenges and Discoveries

The early months of motherhood were a transformative period for Kim. With Quincy's arrival, every day was a journey of learning and growth that required dedication, patience, and a considerable amount of adjustment. The role of a mother presented continuous challenges, but it also brought a joy she had never known. Each small gesture, each of Quincy's smiles, deepened her profound and unconditional love, giving her the strength to face daily responsibilities.

In difficult moments, Kim drew on her mother's teachings, recalling the words and advice Sarah had always offered. These teachings now served as a valuable guide to navigating the uncertainties and fears tied to her new role. She found comfort in those family bonds that gave her a sense of security and made her feel less alone in such an unfamiliar journey.

Al, too, made an effort to be present, supporting her in the small daily moments and sharing the joys and challenges of their new family adventure. The presence and support of her family became a solid foundation on which to build a new life, filled with precious moments that would remain etched in their hearts.

The first months of motherhood transformed Kim, making her a more self-aware and complete woman. Every day was an opportunity to discover new facets of herself and her love for Quincy, learning to balance dreams and responsibilities with renewed serenity.

A New Balance Between Professional and Family Life

After Quincy's birth in 1991, Kim found herself balancing the responsibilities of motherhood with her professional ambitions. Determined not to give up on her dreams, she began to build a balance between family life and her career in fashion. This period tested her strength and resilience, pushing her to reconcile her goals with her son's needs.

In 1992, Kim resumed her work as a model, participating in runway shows and photoshoots. Her presence in the industry continued to grow, and her determination allowed her to face each challenge head-on. Time management became essential—her days were divided between work commitments and moments dedicated to Quincy, ensuring he received the love and attention he needed.

Her mother, Sarah, provided crucial support. Sarah temporarily moved to New York to help care for Quincy, enabling Kim to continue her career. This familial support strengthened ties across generations and gave Kim the peace of mind to pursue her goals with renewed energy.

Yet, maintaining a balance between professional and personal life was no simple task. The demands of the fashion industry required frequent travel and unpredictable schedules, testing Kim's ability to manage both spheres. Her determination and desire to create a stable future for Quincy pushed her to persevere.

This transitional period represented a phase of personal growth for Kim. She learned to manage priorities, to delegate when necessary, and to value quality time with her son. These experiences prepared her to face greater challenges, including the eventual end of her relationship with Al B. Sure! and the subsequent period of transformation that would bring new changes and opportunities.

An Inevitable Crisis: The Pain of Separation

Over time, the relationship between Kim and Al began to show cracks. At first, their connection had seemed unbreakable, built on affinity and passion, but the pressures of their public lives and differences in priorities gradually surfaced. Kim longed for stability that extended beyond life in the spotlight, while Al, fully immersed in his successful music career, seemed increasingly distant, distracted by the fast-paced rhythms and temptations that surrounded him.

Gradually, Kim discovered that Al was often drawn into flings and superficial affairs, betraying her trust more than once. Each new revelation felt like a wound reopening, leaving her to face the disappointment and humiliation alone. Despite the hurt, she tried to hold onto their bond for Quincy's sake and out of respect for the life they had built together. Yet, each act of infidelity reminded her of how much Al had changed and how their relationship was crumbling under the weight of mistrust.

Nights spent alone grew more frequent, and Kim found herself questioning whether she could truly endure such a wounded love. Al's attempts to regain her trust clashed with the harsh reality of a hurt that refused to heal. Even when he tried to show remorse, she felt unable to ignore the signs that their love—once everything to her—was reaching its end.

In the end, with deep sadness but a clear sense of what was best for herself and Quincy, Kim decided to close this chapter. Their farewell was painful, a definitive break bearing the weight of broken promises and a love that could no longer be salvaged. Both felt the emptiness left by the end of their story, but Kim walked away with a new sense of strength, determined to build a life founded on respect and sincerity.

Chapter 6: A New Relationship with Sean "Diddy" Combs

A Meeting Destined to Change the Future

Kim Porter and Sean "Diddy" Combs first crossed paths in 1994, a pivotal moment for both of them. Kim was striving to build a new life for herself and her son Quincy, while Diddy was emerging as a powerhouse in the music industry, already known for his determination and revolutionary vision. When their eyes met for the first time, there was an immediate attraction—a spark that held a promise of change. Yet, along with her interest, Kim felt a sense of caution.

Having experienced a relationship with Al B. Sure!, Kim understood the delicate balance between love and sacrifice, between passion and vulnerability. This encounter with Diddy fascinated and intrigued her, but it also reminded her that opening her heart again would require courage. She saw in him an ambitious man capable of making a difference in the world, but she was also aware that this bond might plunge her into a whirlwind of visibility, fame, and inevitable challenges.

Over the following weeks, Kim and Diddy spent more and more time together, cultivating a connection that proved deep and genuine. Their time together was filled with laughter, open conversations, and shared dreams. Despite her initial fear, Kim found herself wanting to explore this new relationship, working to overcome past wounds and opening herself to the possibility of building something stable and sincere. Her natural caution became a strength—a guide that allowed her to approach this new beginning with maturity and awareness.

Kim saw the potential for a shared life that went beyond romance, one that also represented a path of mutual growth. Those early meetings laid the foundation for a love story that would become one of the most significant chapters in her life. This was only the beginning of a relationship that would redefine their lives, marking the start of a new phase rich with hope and promise.

A Deep and Conscious Connection

As their relationship progressed, Kim and Diddy found themselves building a unique bond grounded in deep, mutual understanding. Both had lived through formative experiences that made them appreciate the value of an authentic connection. For Kim, the start of this love story was unlike her past relationships; alongside Diddy, she felt she could fully express herself and be seen for who she truly was.

Their bond developed gradually, leaving room for honesty and respect. Diddy admired Kim's inner strength and her ability to stay true to herself, while she saw in him not only a charismatic figure but a man with whom she could build something real. They were drawn together not only by attraction but by a shared desire to grow, support each other, and respect each other's spaces and challenges.

This connection led them both to mature, to view their relationship not as a mere chapter in their lives but as a solid foundation on which they could rest their dreams and future plans. It was a relationship that, in its simplicity, promised to be lasting and meaningful.

A New World of Opportunities and Challenges

Being by the side of one of the most influential figures in the music world opened a new dimension of visibility and opportunity for Kim but also brought continuous pressures and challenges. Her relationship with Diddy introduced her to a realm beyond the fashion world, drawing her into show business with all its allure and complexities. Kim often found herself attending prestigious events, meeting prominent figures in the music industry, and constantly being in the public eye.

This was an opportunity for Kim to explore new dimensions of her career and grow alongside someone who shared her ambition and desire for success. However, these new possibilities also brought responsibilities she had never faced before. Being with Diddy meant living under constant media scrutiny, with every move observed and often amplified. Kim had to learn to handle the pressures of public attention, finding a balance between her private life and public image.

This period demanded a great deal of adaptability from her, along with inner strength to preserve her identity in a world that often consumes people. Her relationship with Diddy became both a chance for growth and a test of their bond. In this new world, Kim discovered strengths she hadn't known she possessed, facing each challenge with determination and learning to value opportunities without losing herself.

Building Trust in a Public Sphere

Kim and Diddy's relationship developed under the watchful eye of the media, and maintaining a genuine bond in such a public space required steady, unbreakable trust. They both knew that every gesture would be observed and interpreted—sometimes misinterpreted—which posed a continual challenge. For Kim, who yearned for a deep and stable connection, learning to navigate this level of exposure was essential to protect what they had.

Facing public pressure together required delicate balance. Kim and Diddy committed to preserving their private life, finding moments away from the spotlight where they could nurture true intimacy. Maintaining their authenticity in such a complex setting was a testament to their mutual strength and trust. Kim demonstrated a remarkable ability to adapt, learning to live with the media buzz and transforming it into a shield that protected their relationship.

This period only served to strengthen their bond, as every public challenge overcome became a building block cementing their union. Kim and Diddy managed to build a stable relationship, finding strength in mutual trust to face a world that often tried to disrupt their peace.

Kim's Role as a Guide and Support

In her relationship with Diddy, Kim was more than just a partner; she was a key reference point, a guide who offered support during times of pressure. Her stability and ability to stay centered provided him with balance in an often chaotic and competitive world. Kim's gentle yet steadfast strength helped Diddy navigate the complexities of fame, reminding him of the importance of preserving a protected personal space.

While Diddy was busy building his music empire, he found in Kim a valuable support—a person who understood the difficulties of success and offered him a fresh perspective. Kim's sensitivity and wisdom allowed her to bring him back to reality, helping him reflect on his choices and assess his priorities. This support was not only emotional but also practical; Kim often became the calm, reassuring voice during intense moments, a stable and discreet presence that allowed Diddy to stay focused on his goals.

Kim's role as a guide and support did not go unnoticed. Together, they built a solid relationship in which each could lean on the other. Her ability to remain true to her values and offer support without overstepping gave Diddy the strength to face the most challenging moments in his career.

Kim's Drive for a Stable Family

Despite the fast-paced life alongside Diddy, Kim had a deep desire to build a stable family—an environment rooted in love and respect. Her upbringing, in a family that had instilled strong values, inspired her to seek a balanced life, not only for herself but for the children she dreamed of having. With Diddy, Kim felt that this vision could become a reality.

Throughout their relationship, Kim openly shared with Diddy her vision of a future together, a life founded on family stability and mutual support. The presence of Quincy, her son from her previous relationship, served as a constant reminder of the kind of love and care she wanted to continue fostering. This drive toward a solid family was a guiding force for Kim, motivating her to consistently build a serene and secure environment for herself and her loved ones.

Kim saw their relationship as not only a love story but a life project, a path that would allow them to grow as individuals and as a family. Her desire for a united, stable family became a key foundation of their bond—a shared dream that would shape their choices and represent, for both of them, a promise for the future.

Diddy's Special Bond with Quincy

During his relationship with Kim, Diddy developed a deep and meaningful bond with Quincy, Kim's son from her previous relationship with Al B. Sure! From the start, Diddy showed himself to be present and willing, building a relationship based on respect and mutual affection. For Quincy, Diddy was not just a successful public figure but someone genuine and caring, capable of offering support and guidance.

For Diddy, his bond with Quincy was something truly special. Although Quincy was not his biological son, Diddy felt a strong responsibility and wanted to be a stable guide in his life. Kim watched with gratitude and pride as Diddy dedicated himself to becoming a positive role model for Quincy, contributing to his growth and being present throughout the milestones of his childhood. The time they spent together, even in the simplest of settings, strengthened this bond and showed just how deeply Diddy cared for the boy's happiness and well-being.

This special connection further solidified Kim and Diddy's relationship. For Kim, seeing Diddy's involvement in Quincy's life was a confirmation of his desire to build a united family. Over time, Diddy became a father figure to Quincy—a reliable presence he could depend on, forming a bond that went beyond simply being his mother's partner.

Growing Together Through Challenges and Compromises

Their relationship was not without its challenges; in fact, it was during difficult times that their bond grew strongest. Both were pursuing ambitious careers, and balancing these with their life as a couple required compromise and adaptability. With her patient and resilient temperament, Kim learned to understand the pressures her partner faced and aimed to offer her support without sacrificing her own identity.

Diddy, in turn, worked to balance the demands of his career with those of the family they were building. Every challenge overcome, every compromise found, became an opportunity for mutual growth. For them, the key to success lay in maintaining open and honest communication and understanding that harmony as a couple required dedication from both sides.

This ability to face difficulties together and support each other in times of uncertainty provided a solid foundation for their relationship. The trials and sacrifices transformed their bond into a partnership of deep understanding—an alliance that, despite the challenges, brought them closer each day.

A Love That Becomes Part of Public Life

As time passed, Kim and Diddy's relationship became increasingly visible to the world. The couple began attending public events together, presenting themselves not only as two successful figures but as a symbol of unity and genuine affection. Each appearance was a celebration of their connection, and the public welcomed them enthusiastically, seeing in them a perfect blend of charisma and authenticity.

They attended fashion shows, galas, and important events, sharing their love story with the world, fully aware of the expectations and attention this brought. Although they always kept part of their lives private, they managed to transform their bond into a lasting presence in the pop culture landscape of the time, becoming, for many, an example of balance and strength.

Yet this exposure was not without its difficulties. Being in the spotlight meant facing speculations and pressures, but both displayed a remarkable ability to remain true to themselves. Each event they attended became an opportunity to show that their relationship was built on a solid foundation, where mutual respect and closeness were evident to anyone watching.

Preparing for the Future as a Couple and Family

With their relationship growing stronger and more visible, Kim and Diddy began to shape a shared vision of the future. The couple, now firmly established in the public eye, reflected on the possibility of expanding their family, marking the beginning of a new phase in their life together. The values they had built their relationship on—respect, mutual support, and authenticity—formed the basis for a life plan that extended beyond romance, aiming for a united and stable family.

For Kim, who had always dreamed of a solid family, this journey felt like a profound realization of their bond. The knowledge that she had a partner committed to the same goals gave her confidence and peace. For Diddy, too, the idea of growing as a father figure and creating a stable foundation was becoming increasingly meaningful, solidifying his dedication to Kim and the plans that were beginning to take shape for them.

This vision led them to enthusiastically and carefully prepare for the next chapter of their story: the arrival of their first child together and the growth of their family. With the birth of Christian, they would embrace new responsibilities and explore the experience of parenthood with a closeness that had deep roots.

Chapter 7: Christian's Birth and Family Growth

A Joyful Announcement: Kim's Pregnancy

When Kim discovered she was pregnant with Diddy's child, it was a moment of immense joy and new hopes for the future. This news marked not just the possibility of new life but also a chance to build a stable and loving family. During those years of success and challenges, they saw this upcoming arrival as a fresh perspective that went beyond careers and fame.

The announcement brought happiness to their lives and those around them. For Kim, becoming a mother was the fulfillment of a deep wish, cultivated since childhood. Her relationship with her mother, Sarah, had taught her the value of care and family love, and she felt it was time to pass those values to her own child.

Throughout the pregnancy, Kim prepared thoughtfully and with care. Each day was an opportunity to dream and envision the future, imagining the environment she wanted to create for her child. This pregnancy symbolized renewal and strength for the couple, representing a shared project that signaled a new stage of commitment and growth. It was the beginning of an adventure that would deeply shape their lives and bring with it a new and unconditional love.

Diddy's Devotion and Growing Bond with Kim

During the pregnancy, Sean "Diddy" Combs showed special dedication to Kim, strengthening their bond as they awaited the arrival of their first child together. In 1997, while Diddy's music career was peaking with the release of *No Way Out*, featuring the hit "I'll Be Missing You" in memory of his friend The Notorious B.I.G., he ensured that Kim felt loved and supported, actively participating in medical visits and preparations.

Their connection grew as they shared quiet moments away from the spotlight, like peaceful walks and evenings at home, allowing them to connect more deeply. Diddy, known for his energy and ambition, revealed a gentler, more reflective side, working to create a calm environment for Kim and their future child.

This phase highlighted their ability to balance external pressures with family importance, laying the foundation for a deeper, lasting bond.

Preparing to Welcome Christian

As Christian's birth approached, Kim and Diddy eagerly prepared to welcome him. Pregnancy represented not just a new phase for their relationship but also an opportunity to create a safe, loving space for their child. Despite work obligations, Diddy found time to join these special moments, reflecting his strong desire to build a united family.

Kim, with her experience as Quincy's mother, paid attention to every detail, from selecting a crib to choosing nursery colors. She wanted each element to reflect the love and care with which they were preparing for Christian's arrival. Diddy, in turn, stayed present during shopping and medical appointments, providing Kim with constant support.

These moments of anticipation, involving friends and family, made the waiting period even more exciting. The couple shared dreams and hopes for the future, imagining life once Christian arrived. This phase not only strengthened their bond but also set the foundation for the family environment they wanted to create together.

The Birth of Christian: Indescribable Joy

On April 4, 1998, Kim Porter and Sean "Diddy" Combs joyfully welcomed their first child together, Christian Casey

Combs. This moment was pure happiness for Kim, who felt complete and empowered as a mother holding her son for the first time. Christian's birth marked not just family expansion but also a deeper connection between Kim and Diddy, united in the shared responsibilities and joys of parenthood.

At that time, Diddy was at the peak of his music career, with *No Way Out* achieving tremendous success. Despite professional demands, he lovingly embraced his new role as a father, supporting Kim and actively caring for their newborn. Together, they aimed to create a peaceful, loving family environment, balancing public life with private needs.

Christian's arrival brought a new dynamic, with Quincy, Kim's son from her previous relationship with Al B. Sure!, enthusiastically welcoming his younger brother. Kim focused on nurturing a strong bond between the two, ensuring they both felt loved and valued. This event was a milestone in their journey together, further strengthening their commitment to family.

Kim's Role as Mother to Quincy and Christian

Following Christian's birth, Kim faced the challenge of raising a blended family, balancing Quincy's needs with those of the newborn. Quincy, born in 1991 from Kim's previous relationship, was already used to sharing his mother with her demanding career, but the arrival of a sibling introduced a new family dynamic.

Kim was devoted to fostering a strong bond between the two brothers, encouraging moments of closeness and creating spaces where both could feel important. Her days were a careful balance between caring for baby Christian and spending quality time with Quincy, supporting him in his early interests and passions. For Kim, it was essential that both boys felt loved and appreciated, regardless of family background.

Through simple activities and special moments, Kim instilled in Quincy and Christian values she held dear: mutual respect, family support, and cultural heritage. Her dedication to creating a stable, harmonious environment allowed her to maintain a united family capable of facing the challenges of public life without forgetting the essence of family bonds.

Diddy's Role as a Father Figure to Quincy

Over time, Diddy developed a strong connection with Quincy. Although not Quincy's biological father, Diddy worked to be a positive, consistent presence, a role model Quincy could rely on. Diddy wanted to provide support and encouragement, aware of the importance of having a stable figure in Quincy's life.

Between Quincy and this new paternal figure, a relationship of trust and respect grew. Their time together became meaningful, offering opportunities to share essential values and future aspirations. Kim, grateful and proud, watched as this relationship strengthened day by day.

This special bond became an anchor for Quincy, contributing to the family's overall harmony and stability. Their commitment to building a united, loving family manifested in these daily interactions, proving that they were creating a family foundation capable of embracing and valuing each member with warmth and understanding.

Creating a United, Peaceful Home

With Christian's arrival and Quincy's inclusion in the family, Kim committed to building a serene environment where family bonds were a source of stability and love. She wanted her children to grow up feeling valued and protected in a home where each could find comfort and security. Aware of the challenges of a blended family, she handled each situation with patience and maternal intuition, finding creative ways to foster harmony.

Kim encouraged Quincy and Christian to share moments, creating opportunities to strengthen their bond. Everyday activities, like family nights or park outings, were precious moments for Kim to teach the importance of family and mutual affection. Each small gesture, every word of encouragement, contributed to creating a sense of belonging and peace that she so deeply desired for them.

Diddy shared this vision, and together they worked to protect their family's privacy from external pressures, maintaining calm despite public attention. Kim was dedicated to providing her children with an upbringing rooted in values and respect, instilling in them the confidence to face the world, knowing they always had a safe home to return to.

The Challenges of Managing a Family in the Public Eye

Maintaining a stable, protected family life was no easy task for Kim and Diddy, given the constant media attention. As public figures, their everyday lives often became subjects of interest, complicating efforts to create a normal routine for their children. The couple, however, was determined to safeguard the children's privacy, shielding them from the exposure that could impact their childhood.

For Kim, this challenge required a delicate balance between her career and motherhood. She wanted Quincy and Christian to have a peaceful childhood, free from external pressures, where they could grow and experience life without the burden of their parents' fame. Though difficulties arose, she approached each situation with calm and determination, working tirelessly to create a secure family environment.

Diddy, aware of the complexities of their lifestyle, supported Kim's efforts. Together, they aimed to provide a normal childhood for their children, with simple gestures and a constant presence, like family playtime and outings away from the spotlight. These efforts helped the couple build a solid family unit, a haven of calm where their children could grow safely despite the surrounding fame.

Moments of Family Joy and Connection

Despite the challenges of keeping their family life private, Kim and Diddy succeeded in creating moments of genuine joy and connection with Quincy and Christian. In these private spaces, they focused on building memories to strengthen family bonds, from simple dinners together to evenings filled with laughter and play. Their home became a safe haven, where each daily gesture was an opportunity to nurture love and closeness among parents and children.

Kim, with her knack for creating a welcoming, loving atmosphere, found in small, everyday moments the key to family unity. She organized creative afternoons, imaginative games for the children, and family movie nights that became traditions. Through these simple acts, Kim fostered a sense of belonging in her children, giving them a place where they could simply be themselves, away from the external clamor.

Diddy contributed with his joyful spirit and desire to impart the importance of family values. Despite his busy schedule, he always made time for special moments when the family could bond through fun activities. The children grew up secure in the knowledge that they had two parents who supported them unconditionally, providing them with stability and unwavering love.

These moments of connection embodied the essence of family for Kim and Diddy: a source of strength and inspiration that helped them face challenges and keep their core values alive.

A Bond That Grows Beyond Differences

Over the years, Kim and Diddy's family solidified as a strong, harmonious unit capable of overcoming the typical challenges of blended families. Kim's sensitivity and dedication created an environment where each family member felt accepted and loved, regardless of origins and differences. Christian's birth had strengthened this unity, giving Quincy a brother to share experiences and grow with, forming a bond that transcended biological ties.

Kim felt a profound sense of responsibility toward her children, ensuring that both received equal love and attention, leaving no room for jealousy or inequality. Every family occasion was an opportunity to foster mutual understanding and harmony, instilling in the children the values of solidarity and respect. Their home was a place of open dialogue, where everyone could express their thoughts and feelings, thus strengthening family bonds.

Inspired by Kim's dedication, Diddy actively supported this approach, working to build relationships with Quincy and Christian that valued each boy's individuality. Together, they created a unique family environment where diversity was celebrated as a strength, shaping their children's characters and teaching them the beauty of a blended family.

Kim and Diddy's ability to integrate differences and build a family based on genuine values represented one of the most significant achievements of their relationship. They had created a network of affection and support where the children could grow confidently, secure in belonging to a strong, united family ready to support each other in any circumstance.

Chapter 8: Temporary Crisis, Reconciliation, and the Birth of the Twins

The Burden of Commitments and Differences

In 2006, the relationship between Kim Porter and Sean "Diddy" Combs hit a challenging phase. Diddy's commitments to his music career and Kim's responsibilities as a mother and model led to a growing distance between them. Differences in priorities and expectations began to surface, testing the strength of their bond.

Kim sensed that the balance in their relationship was wavering. Diddy's frequent absences left a void in family life, making her question the possibility of maintaining a stable and deep connection. Meanwhile, Diddy struggled to reconcile his professional ambitions with family responsibilities, feeling the weight of both public and private expectations.

This period of crisis pushed both to reflect on their priorities and the future of their union. External pressures and personal differences became more evident, requiring an honest evaluation of their feelings and shared aspirations. Despite the difficulties, this period of crisis offered an opportunity for them to better understand themselves and the value of their relationship, laying the groundwork for future decisions.

Moments of Tension and Misunderstanding

As their differing perspectives and life rhythms became more pronounced, tension grew. Diddy's extended absences due to his career and record label responsibilities weighed heavily on their relationship. Kim, seeking more stability, often found herself handling the family's daily challenges alone, yearning for a stronger sense of balance.

The distance led to misunderstandings that chipped away at their intimacy. Diddy felt torn between pursuing success and acknowledging his family's needs. Meanwhile, Kim began contemplating her future and her priorities as a mother and partner. These conflicts, though painful, brought about introspection for both.

Their differences often erupted in heated arguments, revealing insecurities and pent-up dissatisfaction. Their once solid relationship now seemed strained by the struggle to reconcile their visions. However, despite the turmoil, both were determined to find a solution, recognizing that their connection was vital for themselves and their children. Their shared commitment to preserving the family laid the foundation for a future reconciliation.

A Difficult Decision: Temporary Separation

In the latter half of 2006, the tensions between Kim and Diddy peaked, leading to the difficult decision to temporarily separate. Already strained by work obligations and personal differences, Kim discovered that Diddy had fathered a daughter, Chance, with another woman, Sarah Chapman. This revelation was a harsh blow, leaving her feeling deeply betrayed and disappointed. Distance became increasingly appealing, both to give each other space to reflect and to protect herself and her children.

During this separation, Kim moved temporarily to Los Angeles with the children, seeking refuge from the public eye and situations that felt destabilizing. This was a complex period marked by solitude and reflection for both. Kim, as a mother, contemplated the future she wanted to build for her children, with a focus on family balance that she was unwilling to compromise.

Diddy, in his own isolation, was forced to examine his actions and consider the sacrifices needed to reconcile his personal ambitions with family responsibilities. The distance and temporary separation became an opportunity for both to clarify their feelings and decide if their bond was strong enough to withstand time and difficulty. Underlying it all, the desire to remain a united family persisted, and this pause would become the turning point for a conscious and genuine reconciliation.

The Discovery of an Unbreakable Bond

During the separation, Kim and Diddy had the chance to reflect deeply on their relationship and shared feelings. Although painful, the distance revealed the strength of their connection, which went beyond misunderstandings and past mistakes. Both realized that, despite challenges and differences, there was genuine affection and a shared desire to build a unified family.

For Kim, time away from Diddy allowed her to rediscover her inner strength and better understand her feelings. She realized she couldn't ignore the special moments and shared experiences nor the enduring connection between them. Diddy, in turn, began to see the true importance of Kim in his life, recognizing her as the balance and stability he had long sought. Their separation underscored a simple yet powerful truth: despite difficulties, their bond was unbreakable.

This period of reflection marked a profound shift in their view of the future. They both realized they wanted to overcome misunderstandings and build a stronger, more authentic relationship. The separation had only strengthened their resolve to be a family ready to face life's challenges together. This period of introspection brought them to a new awareness, paving the way for a future of greater stability and understanding, grounded in mutual respect and love.

To protect the family, Kim was ready to forgive Diddy's indiscretions and move forward.

A New Chapter of Complicity and Stability

After the separation and the reflections that led them to rediscover the value of their bond, Kim and Diddy decided to give their relationship a second chance. Re-entering each other's lives required trust and a willingness to heal old wounds, but both felt it was worth the effort. They reunited with a fresh understanding, committed to building a more mature relationship grounded in mutual respect.

This "new chapter" in their story was built on a more genuine sense of partnership. Kim and Diddy made efforts to communicate openly, working through difficulties without letting misunderstandings or external pressures threaten their bond again. For Kim, the reconciliation was a testament to the commitment and love they both had for the family they were creating. Diddy, in turn, began prioritizing a balance between work and home life, showing his desire to be a present and supportive partner.

This newfound stability allowed the couple to reinforce family ties. For Quincy and Christian, their parents' reconciliation meant growing up in a more peaceful environment where trust and harmony reigned. The renewed partnership between Kim and Diddy not only strengthened their relationship but also laid the groundwork for a more resilient family capable of facing life's challenges together. Their commitment to maintaining this stability would guide them through future steps, especially as new responsibilities approached.

Kim's Pregnancy Announcement: Two New Lives on the Way

Shortly after reconciling, Kim and Diddy received news that would mark the beginning of a new chapter: Kim was pregnant with twins. The discovery brought immense joy, representing an opportunity to further strengthen family bonds. For Kim, the twins' arrival symbolized hope, a gift that would allow her to expand her family in a more stable and peaceful environment.

The pregnancy news was received with great enthusiasm by the entire family. Kim, who had always dreamed of a large family, saw this experience as a chance to create something lasting. Her pregnancy brought a new energy into the home, filling hearts with anticipation and tenderness. Diddy, who had previously divided his time between career and family, began dedicating more time to home life, preparing attentively for the twins' arrival.

During this period, Kim found comfort in her mother Sarah's support and advice. Quincy and Christian, excited to become older brothers, joined in the preparations, making this moment even more special. Together, Kim and Diddy lovingly focused on the details of the new lives ahead, sharing each step and creating a warm, supportive atmosphere. The twins' arrival represented new hope for Kim and Diddy, a sign that, despite past difficulties, their union was ready to embrace a future filled with promise.

Preparing for the Twins' Arrival

With the news of the twin pregnancy, Kim and Diddy began preparing for the next chapter in their family life. This time, the couple chose to take all the time they needed to welcome the new arrivals with the utmost attention and calm. The home was filled with love and anticipation, transforming every corner to welcome the twins, making the wait a special shared experience.

Kim dedicated most of her days to preparations, carefully selecting everything the babies would need. Every detail— from matching outfits to twin cribs—was chosen with love, creating a warm and protective environment. For her, these moments were an opportunity to bring her vision of family to life, coming closer to the dream of a united and stable family unit.

Diddy, who had previously devoted much energy to his career, began balancing his commitments better to be present during key moments of the pregnancy. He attended medical appointments and supported Kim in every way possible. For him, the twins' arrival was a chance to renew his commitment to the family, to atone for past indiscretions, and to build a home filled with love and security for their children.

Quincy and Christian also joined in the preparations, showing enthusiasm and curiosity about their future sisters. Kim involved the boys in small tasks, explaining the importance of mutual support and reinforcing their sense of belonging. This collective anticipation made the family stronger, ready to face change together and united by affection and the shared goal of building a solid, lasting future.

The atmosphere of love and unity felt at home was the realization of a dream for Kim, a vision that had transcended obstacles. Every moment in this phase became a precious memory, and every smile and preparation fueled the couple's belief in their ability to face the joys and responsibilities of their new family life.

The Birth of D'Lila Star and Jessie James: A Dream Realized

December 21, 2006, was a day of indescribable joy for Kim and Diddy, as twin girls D'Lila Star and Jessie James entered the world, bringing a wave of love and happiness. For Kim, holding her daughters for the first time was a moment that exceeded all expectations. Years of hope and dreams had materialized, making every past sacrifice a distant memory. The family she had longed for was now a reality.

68

Their birth brought renewed energy into family life. Kim dedicated herself lovingly to the newborns, getting to know them day by day and establishing a nurturing routine that strengthened their bond. The sleepless nights and moments of fatigue were outweighed by the babies' smiles, which embodied life's beauty and innocence. Her experience as a mother took on new dimensions, leaving her feeling fulfilled.

Diddy, thrilled by his daughters' birth, was committed to being present at every stage of their development. He built a special relationship with them, participating in family life and offering Kim his support. The twins symbolized a renewed sense of responsibility for him, a reminder of the importance of balancing career and family. Together, Kim and Diddy found inspiration and joy in their daughters, giving meaning to every effort.

This new phase brought the entire family closer. Quincy and Christian, delighted by the arrival of their sisters, grew even closer to Kim and Diddy, joining in family life with enthusiasm. Each day became an opportunity to strengthen bonds and create precious memories, turning their home into a haven of love and serenity. For Kim, with D'Lila Star and Jessie James, her life felt complete, as if each piece of the puzzle had finally fallen into place.

Facing the Challenge of Raising Four Children

With D'Lila Star and Jessie James's arrival, Kim and Diddy's family became even more dynamic. Now with four children, Kim faced the challenge of balancing each child's unique needs and personalities, ensuring that everyone received the necessary attention and love. Managing such a large family wasn't easy, but Kim tackled each day with dedication and love, making each child feel her constant, reassuring presence.

Family life required enormous commitment. Kim carefully organized their days, balancing household duties with the children's activities. Each child had their own interests and passions: Quincy was drawn to art and music, while Christian, the most spirited, showed curiosity about his father's career. The twins, still young, were a world to explore, and Kim made a point of spending exclusive time with each of them, building lasting connections.

Life under the spotlight added constant pressure, but the reunited couple prioritized protecting their children from unwanted attention, maintaining family privacy as an essential goal. This challenge required patience and resolve, but for Kim, nothing was more important than giving her children a serene, as-normal-as-possible childhood, despite their parents' fame. Each day, with love and resilience, she faced family life's demands, turning their home into a safe haven where every child could grow and thrive.

Challenges Reemerge

The increasing parental responsibilities, coupled with Diddy's professional commitments that often kept him away, began creating emotional distance between them. Kim, devoted to her children's care, found herself managing many daily challenges alone, which deepened her sense of isolation. Differences in priorities and expectations weighed on their relationship, leading to misunderstandings and frustrations.

Despite their efforts to maintain a united front, cracks in their relationship became more apparent. The pressures of living in the public eye and rumors of infidelity intensified the strain. Kim and Diddy found themselves at a crossroads, forced to confront their relationship's realities and consider their family's future.

This period of turbulence marked the beginning of a reflective phase, prompting them to evaluate their needs and prioritize their children's well-being. The path to family peace proved more complex than expected, requiring difficult decisions and a renewed commitment for the collective good.

Chapter 9: The Final Separation and Co-Parenting with Diddy

A Period of Growing Tensions

Though the arrival of the twins initially strengthened Kim and Diddy's bond, the increasing demands of Diddy's career and the responsibility of managing a large family began creating a widening rift. Diddy was deeply engaged in his expanding career and numerous projects that kept him frequently away, while Kim, focused on the children's well-being, faced many of the daily challenges on her own.

The distance between them wasn't just physical; it was emotional as well. Kim felt that the weight of their blended family rested almost entirely on her shoulders. Despite the support of friends and family, feelings of isolation grew stronger, and she often longed for a balance that seemed increasingly out of reach. Diddy, on the other hand, struggled to reconcile his ambition in the entertainment world with the awareness that his absence was impacting family life.

Differences in priorities and the fast-paced demands of life in the spotlight began to strain their relationship. Misunderstandings that were once handled with patience now accumulated without resolution. Although both were motivated to preserve the family, the unrelenting tensions made it clear that maintaining stability was an increasing challenge. This period marked a time of reflection, leading them to question what was truly best for themselves and their children.

The Decision to Go Separate Ways

After months of tension and attempts at reconciliation, Kim and Diddy came to a difficult yet inevitable decision: to separate permanently. In 2007, aware of the insurmountable differences between them, they realized that staying together had become more challenging than ever. Despite shared memories and genuine affection, the complexity of their relationship forced them to consider realistically what was best for their family and, above all, their children. Kim, who had always envisioned a stable, harmonious family, acknowledged that the tensions had eroded their bond beyond repair.

The decision was not taken lightly. Kim still cared deeply for Diddy and had invested much in their relationship, hoping their differences could be resolved. However, after repeated attempts, she realized the emotional cost of staying together was too high, especially for the children, who needed a peaceful and stable environment. Diddy, though reluctant, understood that separation could be a responsible choice, allowing them both to find their paths while shielding the children from family conflicts.

This decision marked the start of a new phase. Kim, with courage, accepted the reality and prepared to rebuild her life with a focus on herself and her children. For her, stepping away from Diddy also meant rediscovering her own identity and independence—qualities she felt she had set aside for the family's sake. Diddy, in turn, was forced to reflect on his mistakes and priorities, committing to remain a stable presence for the children despite the end of their relationship.

While the separation represented the closing of an important chapter, it also opened the door to a new family dynamic in which they would continue to be present as co-parents, placing the children's well-being above all else.

Coping with the Pain of Separation

Although the separation was a mutual and conscious decision, for Kim, dealing with the separation from Diddy was deeply painful. The end of such a significant relationship was not only the closure of a life chapter but also the necessity to reorganize everything she had built and adjust to a new reality. For years, she had hoped to provide her children with a united and stable family, and accepting that this vision had shattered left her with a profound sense of sadness and failure.

The separation process gave Kim the chance to reflect on her choices and on what she truly desired for herself and her children. Facing life alone again, she confronted intense, conflicting emotions: on one hand, the regret for a relationship she had hoped would last; on the other, the need to reclaim her independence and build family stability without Diddy. Kim spent a lot of time reflecting, processing her pain in a constructive way, turning it into newfound inner strength.

For Diddy, too, the separation brought a period of introspection. Though accustomed to a fast-paced life and public relationships, he felt the impact of distance from his family and of his choices. Over time, they both realized that while their relationship as a couple had ended, their commitment as parents remained. For Kim, this was a new opportunity for personal and maternal growth, restoring her emotional stability and strength to move forward.

Though not without moments of sadness, the separation also marked a rebirth for Kim. Over time, she learned to accept the past and look to the future with hope. Her children remained her greatest motivation, and despite the challenges of a new life, she devoted herself to them with even more love and determination. This journey of healing allowed her to rediscover her own worth and understand that, even alone, she could create a safe, nurturing environment for her beloved family.

A Shared Commitment to the Children

Despite the separation, the former couple remained deeply committed to their roles as parents. Determined to provide their children with the stability and love they needed, they recognized the importance of a peaceful and secure environment for Quincy, Christian, and the twins D'Lila Star and Jessie James. They chose to meet this challenge with maturity and mutual respect, establishing a co-parenting foundation based on cooperation.

For Kim, the children were her top priority. She dedicated time and attention to each, ensuring no one felt neglected or impacted by the family's new situation. Her days were filled with close moments with the children, from daily routines to intimate conversations that helped them express their feelings. Despite his busy career, Diddy made an effort to maintain a constant presence in his children's lives. Though his work required frequent travel, he made it a point to be there for important milestones, showing his love and support.

Kim and Diddy's co-parenting became a model of respect and responsibility, a connection that went beyond personal differences. They strove to attend school events, sports activities, and family celebrations together, demonstrating to the children that despite the separation, family remained a fundamental value. For the kids, having both parents present was a source of security and stability, helping them navigate the change without trauma.

Over time, Kim and Diddy built a relationship that not only allowed their children to grow up in a calm environment but also offered a model of cooperation and mutual respect. This new family dynamic, grounded in love and support, showed that even without a romantic relationship, they could remain a united family. For Kim, each sacrifice was worth it, seeing the joy in her children's smiles, and for Diddy, the commitment to being a present father became a source of pride.

Building a New Family Structure

Kim went beyond simply being physically present for the children; she cultivated a unique and genuine relationship with each one. Every child, with their individual personalities, received the attention they needed, strengthening their maternal bond and giving them the security they needed. Quincy, now a teenager, was beginning to forge his own identity, and Kim supported him in finding his path. Christian, younger and more spirited, needed different forms of attention, while the twins, still small, brought tender joy to the family, filling the house with laughter.

The new family structure provided the children with balance and gave Kim an opportunity for personal rediscovery. No longer needing to adjust to a romantic partnership, she could focus on herself, finding renewed meaning in her independence. Through co-parenting, she continued collaborating with Diddy but retained her autonomy, ensuring every decision aligned with the children's best interests.

Kim's commitment to building this new life was reflected in the small family traditions she established: special moments shared with the children, like Friday dinners or game nights. These rituals became the family's glue, providing continuity and the warmth of a true refuge. Kim created an environment that, even without Diddy's constant presence, continued to resonate with love and protection, proving that a family could be strong and united in this new context.

A Relationship Founded on Respect and Friendship

In this new phase, Kim and Diddy transformed their bond, transitioning from a romantic relationship to one rooted in respect and friendship. Recognizing the importance of harmonious collaboration for their children's well-being, they committed to building open, sincere communication. This new balance required time and dedication but enabled them to overcome past misunderstandings and forge a more mature connection.

Kim, with her natural empathy, was able to set aside past hurts, focusing on the importance of effective co-parenting. Diddy, recognizing Kim's value as a mother and as an individual, showed renewed respect for her, appreciating her crucial role in their children's lives. This mutual consideration created a peaceful environment in which the children could feel the unity and affection of their parents despite the end of their romantic relationship.

The transition from couple to co-parents and friends was not without challenges. Moments of sadness and nostalgia surfaced, but both Kim and Diddy found the inner strength to face them, always prioritizing their children's well-being. Holidays and family celebrations became opportunities to show that their love for the children transcended personal differences, providing stability and security.

Over time, their relationship solidified, becoming an example of how two people, though on separate paths, could collaborate with maturity and affection for a shared goal. Kim and Diddy demonstrated that friendship and mutual respect could emerge even from the ashes of a finished relationship, creating a new family dynamic founded on unconditional love for their children.

Family Moments of Togetherness

Despite the separation, Kim and Diddy continued to dedicate time to family moments, giving their children opportunities to feel united despite the challenges. Birthdays, Christmas celebrations, and other significant events became precious occasions for Kim and Diddy to show their children that although they were no longer a couple, the love and respect between them remained. These family gatherings aimed to preserve a warm, joyful atmosphere that made the children feel part of a strong, loving family.

Kim, with her maternal heart, ensured that every detail of these occasions was special for Quincy, Christian, and the twins. For her, the children's happiness was paramount, and each celebration was an opportunity to strengthen their bonds, creating memories they would cherish forever. Diddy, despite his busy career, did everything he could to be present and share these moments, showing his children that family was at the center of his life.

For the children, these times of family togetherness were essential. They helped them see that despite circumstances, they could rely on both parents and feel the emotional stability of a harmonious family unit. Kim and Diddy understood the importance of maintaining this sense of belonging, demonstrating to their children that love was not defined by family structure but by the quality of the bonds supporting it.

These shared moments, in addition to being sources of joy, strengthened Kim and Diddy's bond, who saw the value of each sacrifice reflected in their children's smiles. Their determination to maintain family unity proved that their love for their children could overcome any personal differences, creating a safe, loving environment for them to grow. These moments became the glue of a family that, despite its complexities, continued to resonate with affection and dedication.

Diddy's Commitment as a Present Father

Kim deeply appreciated Diddy's commitment as a father. She understood how essential it was for the children to have a present male role model, and she strove to maintain a cooperative, friendly relationship with him. This bond, built on respect and trust, allowed the children to always feel supported and loved by both parents. Diddy, despite his public life, knew when to step back and dedicate himself entirely to family, demonstrating to his children the importance of love and shared time.

Diddy's paternal presence allowed Kim the freedom to pursue her own dreams and explore new professional paths. With Diddy as an ally in co-parenting, Kim found the strength to rediscover her identity and independence. For her, it was time to build a new phase of her life, one where she could express her personality and talents without compromise. While Diddy continued to be a steady, loving father, Kim prepared to explore new opportunities in entertainment and reaffirm herself as both a woman and a professional.

Chapter 10: New Opportunities in the Entertainment World

A Renewed Professional Drive

After her 2007 separation from Diddy, Kim Porter embarked on a path of personal and professional growth, determined to establish an independent career in the entertainment industry. With newfound energy, she began exploring opportunities that would allow her to fully express her talent and passion for the arts.

Initially, Kim focused on her modeling career, collaborating with prestigious brands and appearing in prominent ad campaigns. Her elegance and unique style earned her recognition in the fashion industry, solidifying her reputation as a style icon.

Kim also ventured into acting, taking on roles in film and television. In 2001, she appeared in *The Brothers* as the character Tammy, and in 2006, she starred as Tanya in *The System Within*. These experiences helped her refine her acting skills and expand her presence in entertainment.

In 2011, Kim joined the VH1 television series *Single Ladies*, playing the character Jasmine. This role allowed her to further explore her acting talent and reach a broader audience.

Determined to expand her personal brand, Kim served as executive producer for the 2008 reality show *I Want to Work for Diddy*, showcasing her abilities behind the scenes. Additionally, she participated in charity events and social initiatives, using her platform to support causes she cared about.

Encouraged by her successes, Kim planned new ventures in entertainment, envisioning a path that would provide her with long-term stability and visibility. Her determination and commitment enabled her to build a solid and respected career, independent of her previous relationship with Diddy.

Through these experiences, Kim Porter proved her remarkable ability to reinvent herself and passionately pursue her professional goals, leaving a lasting impact on the entertainment world.

Collaborations with Prestigious Fashion Brands

Following her separation, Kim Porter poured her energy into collaborations in the fashion industry, enhancing her professional profile and public identity. Known for her charisma and natural elegance, she began working with high-profile brands that viewed her as the ideal representation of style and authenticity. Between 2007 and 2011, she appeared in photo and advertising campaigns for prominent brands celebrated for their commitment to classic elegance and natural beauty—qualities that Kim embodied perfectly.

These partnerships not only increased her visibility but also reinforced her image as an icon of style and class. Brands that collaborated with her appreciated the way she represented authentic femininity, far from common stereotypes. Her natural elegance and sincere approach to work made her a beloved figure in both fashion and the public eye. Each project became an opportunity to express her identity and inner strength, qualities that shone through in every shot and campaign.

Kim also began attending exclusive fashion events and was invited to shows by renowned American and international designers. These occasions allowed her not only to expand her professional network but also to solidify her status as a respected figure in fashion. Through these collaborations, she showed that she could move beyond mere image, presenting a vision of herself that reflected her journey and desire for independent affirmation.

Thanks to this period of intense activity, Kim not only strengthened her name in the industry but also started envisioning new avenues for her brand, opening up possibilities that would give her career a fresh direction.

Entering the World of Television

Determined to diversify her career path, Kim Porter explored new opportunities in television, aiming to broaden her influence and express herself beyond fashion. In 2008, she made a major breakthrough by serving as executive producer of the reality show *I Want to Work for Diddy*. The show followed candidates competing for a job with Diddy, allowing Kim to gain behind-the-scenes experience and learn about the television production process.

Television provided Kim with a platform to reach a larger audience, showcasing a side of herself beyond the glamour of fashion campaigns. This new experience gave her a deeper understanding of television dynamics and helped her develop production and management skills, which would enrich her career in the years ahead. Through the reality show, Kim not only consolidated her media presence but also began building a reputation as a capable professional willing to take on new challenges.

With the show's success and positive audience feedback, Kim began receiving proposals for additional television projects. This new chapter in entertainment allowed her to showcase her talents and further strengthened her public image as an independent woman capable of adapting to various roles. Through television, Kim Porter proved that her professional dedication knew no limits, finding in this medium a way to leave a lasting mark.

Breakthrough Role on the TV Series Single Ladies

In 2011, Kim Porter took on a new professional challenge that allowed her to showcase her acting skills—a field she was increasingly eager to pursue. That year, she landed a role in VH1's popular TV series *Single Ladies*, a dramedy exploring the lives and relationships of a group of friends in the lively city of Atlanta. As Jasmine, Kim portrayed a sophisticated and charismatic character, capturing the attention of audiences and industry insiders alike.

This role offered her a unique chance for professional growth. Working on a major production set allowed her to explore the nuances of acting, refining her abilities and building greater confidence in front of the camera. Jasmine's character embodied a sophisticated energy that perfectly suited Kim's style, allowing her to convey an authentic part of herself to viewers.

In addition to expanding her experience, this role marked a significant step in establishing her independent professional identity. The opportunity to work alongside talented actors and participate in a series with a wide following gave her greater confidence in her abilities and the potential a television career could offer. For Kim, *Single Ladies* was more than just a job—it was an opportunity to be recognized as an actress and solidify her public image.

This experience opened new doors for the future, allowing her to further explore her acting ambitions. With this success, Kim Porter continued to expand her career, once again demonstrating her ability to adapt to new roles and approach each professional challenge with passion.

Expanding Her Personal Brand

With growing success in both fashion and television, Kim Porter recognized the importance of building a personal brand that would resonate with the public. She decided to expand her presence by exploring initiatives that leveraged her unique image of elegance and authenticity. Kim began attending exclusive fashion events and collaborating with brands that shared her values, becoming the face of campaigns that reflected her natural and sophisticated style.

A central part of her strategy involved carefully selecting collaborations and projects: she worked with brands that promoted female empowerment and individuality, two core aspects of her message. These choices allowed Kim to reinforce her image as an independent icon and strong woman. She didn't just promote products; she ensured that each project reflected her lifestyle and values, creating a more genuine, lasting connection with her followers.

Kim soon extended her brand into the beauty industry, appearing as a guest and speaker at beauty and fashion events and fairs, sharing her insights with aspiring young professionals. These activities bolstered her image and established her as a role model for a new generation of young women. With her inspirational approach, Kim Porter gained the support of new fans and attracted interest from potential partners and collaborators, thereby expanding the reach of her personal brand.

Future Ambitions and New Prospects in the Industry

After years of success and collaborations that cemented her role in fashion and entertainment, Kim Porter began contemplating the next phases of her career and the direction she wanted for her future. With a well-established public image, she started planning new initiatives that would elevate her as a style icon while also allowing her to make an authentic impact. She considered launching fashion lines that reflected her timeless elegance, more structured partnerships in the beauty sector, and possibly becoming involved in projects that combined fashion and philanthropy.

At this time, Kim also reflected on the balance between her public and private lives. On one hand, she felt responsible for being a role model for her followers, embodying independence and determination; on the other, she was increasingly aware of the daily challenges of being a mother, a role that required constant dedication and that she held as a top priority. With four children to care for and a demanding career, Kim began carefully planning her future, considering which choices would allow a harmonious balance between professional achievement and family care.

These reflections led her to think about the ongoing challenges of motherhood, prompting her to seek solutions that would enable her to pursue her ambitions without sacrificing her role as a mother. The balance between public commitments and personal needs became a central theme, laying the groundwork for the next chapter of her journey: navigating the unique, sometimes complex challenges of motherhood and career—a duality that would define her future choices and the way she continued to live her life authentically.

Chapter 11: Balancing Motherhood and Career

Being a Single Mother to Quincy, Christian, D'Lila Star, and Jessie James

Following recent life changes, Kim embraced the challenge of raising her four children independently, determined to provide them with a life full of love and security. Adapting to single motherhood, while a significant shift, became an opportunity for her to strengthen her bond with Quincy, Christian, and her twin daughters, D'Lila Star and Jessie James. Every morning, Kim woke with a clear goal: to be a strong, present mother who instilled resilience and independence in her children.

Managing a blended family required impeccable organization and meticulous time management. Between school days, extracurricular activities, and moments of leisure, Kim created a routine that allowed each child to feel seen and valued. With Quincy, her eldest, she maintained a close, supportive relationship, guiding him into adulthood with wise counsel and encouragement. For Christian and the twins, she struck a balance between gentleness and firmness, understanding that her example was the cornerstone of their growth.

Kim's dedication extended beyond daily tasks. She sought to be not only a mother but also a role model her children could look up to and draw inspiration from. She made time for each of them, sharing intimate, precious moments that would become a treasured family legacy. Kim's efforts made every child feel unique and loved, teaching them gratitude for family and mutual respect.

In her heart, her priority was to raise strong, self-assured children ready to face the world with confidence. With determination and love, she created a stable, nurturing environment, despite the inevitable challenges. Her ability to balance motherhood with personal and professional demands became a testament to her resilience and adaptability in every situation.

Navigating Co-Parenting Challenges

Though they had taken different paths, Kim and Diddy remained united in their commitment to their children, striving to provide them with a stable and serene life. Co-parenting required consistent communication and clarity, as both parents understood that family well-being depended on harmony and mutual cooperation. For Kim, collaborating with her former partner meant setting aside any differences to focus on a single priority: the emotional support and happiness of their children.

Every decision was carefully considered to respect the needs of Quincy, Christian, D'Lila Star, and Jessie James, and to manage their shared moments harmoniously. Kim and Diddy established shared guidelines for raising and caring for their children, ensuring each step aligned with the family's core values and priorities. This collaboration wasn't without its difficulties, but Kim understood her role extended beyond co-parenting—she was determined to set a positive example, showing her children that love and respect could anchor any relationship, even in complex situations.

Practically, this commitment meant constantly balancing family obligations with professional responsibilities. Kim dedicated her energy to maintaining an organized, stable structure, reassuring Quincy and her other children that, despite the separation, they remained a united family. Her ability to maintain calm and stability, despite challenges, was a testament to her strength and dedication, offering her children an example of resilience to carry forward.

Special Moments of Tenderness with the Twins

With D'Lila Star and Jessie James, Kim built a bond filled with special attentiveness, adapting her dedication to meet the unique needs of two little girls growing up side by side. For Kim, it was essential that both felt valued as individuals and constantly surrounded by love. Through simple, daily moments—playtime, bedtime talks, or leisurely walks—she fostered a warm and protective environment.

Kim understood the importance of balancing her commitments to be present in her daughters' lives. Every word and embrace in those shared moments became a chance to pass on values of kindness and respect, crucial foundations for healthy development. Despite the fast pace of life, she always found time to listen to them and celebrate their little discoveries, creating cherished memories.

The attention she gave each girl not only strengthened their sense of security but also provided a model of unconditional love they would carry with them. Kim crafted a safe haven for her daughters, where they could freely express themselves, knowing their mother would always be there to listen and guide them. This special connection with D'Lila Star and Jessie James enriched their childhood and deepened Kim's understanding of her unique role, balancing her love for her children with her daily responsibilities.

The Challenge of Managing a Large Family

With four children, each with a distinct personality, Kim faced the daily complexity of balancing each one's needs, ensuring everyone felt valued and protected. Managing a large family required significant organizational skills and patience, qualities Kim exhibited naturally, ensuring that every moment spent together was meaningful. For her, each child represented a unique world, with individual desires and needs that called for dedicated attention and understanding.

Kim structured her days to give each child time and space to express themselves, organizing individual and family activities that fostered their development and strengthened family cohesion. Evenings were often devoted to sharing experiences from the day, reinforcing their sense of belonging. Even on the busiest days, Kim found ways to be present for each of them, balancing affection with guidance, aware of how vital it was to provide security and stability.

Being a mother of four required decisions that carefully balanced her role as a parent with her professional goals. Kim was determined never to sacrifice attention to her children for her public commitments, finding ways to be there for key moments in their growth. This dedication enabled her to build strong relationships with each of her children, rooted in trust and respect—qualities she saw as essential for a close-knit family.

Being a Model of Strength and Resilience

For Kim Porter, motherhood extended beyond daily care; it included the responsibility of being a role model of strength and integrity. Aware of the profound influence her choices would have on her children, Kim modeled resilience and determination, facing challenges with adaptability and optimism. Each day, she demonstrated to them that tenacity and the ability to rise after difficulties were invaluable traits to carry forward in life.

The lessons she shared often sprang from her own experiences, which she recounted with sincerity, finding ways to turn even difficult moments into opportunities for growth. She spoke with her children about how she built her career and the determination she had applied to the fashion and entertainment worlds, emphasizing the importance of never giving up on one's dreams. These conversations were more than stories—they were authentic life lessons she imparted to prepare her children for a complex, unpredictable world.

Being a role model also meant embodying compassion and empathy. Kim showed them that strength wasn't only about overcoming personal struggles but also supporting others on their journeys. This approach, which she practiced daily, helped lay a solid foundation for her children's future, guiding them to trust their abilities and view the future with optimism. Her example as a resilient, loving mother became a beacon for Quincy, Christian, and the twins, inspiring them to build their lives with awareness and integrity.

A Life Devoted to Family

Despite her many professional commitments and the challenges of her career, Kim Porter remained firmly focused on her family. Every decision, whether career-related or personal, was driven by her desire to create a peaceful, stable, and loving environment for her children. She understood that building deep, lasting bonds required dedicated time and attention to each child, ensuring that each moment together reinforced their sense of unity and security.

For Kim, family was not only a priority but also a calling. She deeply valued teaching by example and, through her actions, showed her children the importance of resilience, respect, and determination. Her dedication went beyond daily gestures; it was a constant commitment to being a support system and a guiding light on their paths, whatever directions they might choose to follow.

Throughout her children's growth, Kim remained present, building a solid foundation that allowed them to develop confidence and self-esteem. Her goal was not only to protect them from life's difficulties but also to prepare them to live fully, supporting them as they discovered their passions and talents. This perspective, rooted in love and understanding, would continue to shape how Kim related to her children in the years to come.

As time passed, Kim fully embraced her role as a mentor and guide to Quincy, Christian, D'Lila Star, and Jessie James. Her presence as an encouraging, supportive mother enabled her to help them not only pursue their dreams but also make life's crucial choices. This role as a mentor would grow increasingly significant, allowing her to leave an indelible mark on their growth and accompany them in their first steps toward personal fulfillment.

Chapter 12: A Guiding Role for Her Children

Being a Steady Figure for Quincy

As the eldest child, Quincy Jones Brown faced unique challenges, both in his family role and with increasing public visibility. Kim, aware of the pressures and expectations on Quincy, guided him with love and patience as he navigated the path to adulthood, serving as a steady point of reference. For her, Quincy was a source of pride, and her dedication to him was clear in every word of advice and gesture of support.

Kim worked to prepare Quincy not only for a career in entertainment but also for the complexities of life. She taught him the importance of integrity and facing challenges with resilience, regardless of external pressures. Kim encouraged him to explore his passions and forge a path that was authentic to who he truly was. Quincy knew he could count on her as a mentor, and this bond strengthened his confidence and self-assurance.

In addition to being a loving mother, Kim represented professionalism and resilience for Quincy. She shared anecdotes and lessons from her own career, giving him insights into life in the public eye. Their conversations covered a range of topics, from emotional self-management to maintaining a balanced lifestyle. Kim ensured that Quincy had the tools to navigate the entertainment world with confidence, urging him never to lose sight of his authenticity and to remain true to himself.

Kim's presence became a guiding compass for Quincy's growth and personal development, inspiring him to become a responsible individual capable of making a positive impact. Her support and attentiveness were the foundation of their unique relationship, built on open dialogue and a trust that would accompany him in every choice he made.

Encouraging Christian's Artistic Talents

From a young age, Christian Combs displayed a natural talent for fashion and music. Recognizing his potential, Kim devoted herself to nurturing these passions, becoming a trusted guide and a constant source of encouragement. For Kim, this support wasn't just about a career path but about helping Christian discover and embrace his unique gifts, building his confidence along the way.

In their relationship, Kim balanced attentive listening with practical advice to help Christian reach his full potential in the most authentic way. She encouraged him to explore his creative inclinations without fear, urging him to experiment with new sounds, styles, and modes of expression in both music and fashion. Every decision Christian made had Kim's backing, as she guided him toward thoughtful, well-considered choices.

Kim dedicated special time to listen to Christian's progress, whether he was working on a new song or a fashion project. These meaningful moments strengthened their bond and bolstered Christian's self-assurance. Kim wanted her son to understand that true success came from remaining true to himself, respecting his roots, and maintaining humility despite his career's visibility.

Her support became a cornerstone of Christian's artistic and personal growth, providing him with a safe space to express his creativity and embark on a path that was as personal as it was professional. As both a mother and mentor, Kim instilled in him the importance of pursuing his dreams with dedication, awareness, and passion.

Fostering Independence in the Twins

With D'Lila Star and Jessie James, Kim Porter took an approach centered on independence, encouraging them to develop strong individual identities. From a young age, she instilled in the twins the importance of being true to themselves, encouraging them to explore their interests and build healthy self-esteem. In a world that often placed them in the spotlight, Kim wanted to ensure they had the tools to build solid character, capable of withstanding external pressures.

Kim created a growth environment for the twins that promoted freedom of expression and curiosity. She encouraged them to discover what truly fascinated them, giving them the freedom to pursue different interests, whether sports, arts, or playful activities. Kim was convinced that independence was fundamental for balanced growth and that each daughter, while unique, could find support in their sisterly bond.

In daily life, Kim developed small personal rituals with each twin, like bedtime stories or nature walks, so each girl felt heard and valued. These intimate moments reinforced their bond and allowed each twin to feel special and loved. Kim wanted both daughters to grow up with a strong sense of identity, not simply as part of a duo but as individuals with their own worth.

For Kim, raising D'Lila Star and Jessie James also meant preparing them for a conscious life, teaching them that independence was not only the ability to make decisions but also the capacity to assert themselves with grace and determination. Every lesson, every word of encouragement was an invitation to become self-assured individuals ready to face the world with confidence. Kim passed on to the twins the importance of inner strength and the skill of carving out their own space, both within the family and in society.

Teaching the Value of Authenticity and Integrity

Kim Porter firmly believed that authenticity and integrity were essential to building a meaningful, respected life path. She passed on these values to her children through example and conversations that reflected her experiences. For Kim, staying true to oneself was crucial, especially in navigating life's complexities, particularly when exposed to public opinion and its pressures. She knew it was important for her children to learn not to conform to others' expectations but to find and follow their own paths.

Kim defined authenticity not only as sincerity but also as the courage to show vulnerability and one's true self. In every discussion, she helped her children understand that being genuine would positively impact their relationships and, in the long term, their happiness. For her, integrity meant acting in line with one's values, even when it required sacrifices or involved difficult choices.

Kim often shared her experiences to illustrate the importance of these values. She recounted moments in her career when she had to defend her authenticity, even at the cost of certain opportunities. These examples taught her children that staying true to one's values not only garners respect but also shields them from the highs and lows of public life. Kim hoped these lessons would become a foundation for them, reminding them to live with honesty and coherence, never compromising what they believed in.

Through this approach, Kim instilled a deep respect for personal integrity in her children, laying the groundwork for lives built on truth and self-respect.

Navigating Public Visibility with Her Children

The fame surrounding the family was a reality her children had learned to live with from a young age. Constantly being in the spotlight wasn't easy, especially for children and teenagers still finding themselves and building their identities. With her experience in entertainment, Kim understood the difficulties tied to public visibility and worked hard to protect her children from external pressures, teaching them to balance public and private life.

One of Kim's key teachings was discerning what was real from what was just an image. She explained how the media and social networks often presented a partial or distorted version of reality, emphasizing the importance of not being swayed by others' opinions. She encouraged them to see their family as a safe haven, a place where they could be themselves without fear of judgment. Whenever media attention or a challenging situation arose, Kim turned it into a learning opportunity, helping her children develop critical thinking and distinguish between their true selves and their public image.

Kim also did her best to safeguard their privacy, teaching them the importance of setting boundaries and not sharing every detail of their lives. She wanted each child to grow up freely, without feeling constantly watched, and to build authentic relationships without fear of being exploited or judged. She often discussed the importance of maintaining a private space, a place of peace where they could recharge without relying on external validation for self-worth.

Through her guidance, Kim taught her children the art of coexisting with fame without being defined by it. This approach helped them develop strong self-awareness, enabling them to handle public visibility with balance and wisdom, without ever compromising their authenticity.

Sharing Life Experiences as a Model

For Kim Porter, sharing her life experiences with her children was a way to guide them through challenges, making them feel accompanied and supported at every stage of their growth. Having faced both highs and lows, Kim believed that her stories could offer valuable lessons to her children, helping them see that even the toughest situations could be faced with strength and determination. On quiet nights at home, she would often sit with them to discuss the hurdles she had overcome and the choices that had shaped her life.

One story Kim shared frequently was about her early steps in the fashion industry. She spoke of the initial difficulties and feelings of being lost in a competitive, often unkind environment. She recounted how, as a young and inexperienced model, she had to learn to stand up for herself and believe in her abilities, despite criticism and rejections. These stories served as inspiration and a constant reminder of the importance of resilience and self-belief. Kim encouraged her children not to be discouraged by setbacks, reminding them that every step backward could turn into an opportunity for growth.

Even more delicate moments from her personal life became dialogue starters. She openly discussed the difficulties she had faced in her relationships, disappointments, and painful choices. Without going into specifics, she emphasized the importance of learning to let go when a situation became harmful to one's well-being. Her aim was to teach her children that self-love and respecting one's boundaries were essential to building healthy relationships. Her stories were accompanied by practical advice, meant to teach them the art of mutual respect and understanding.

Kim knew her children would also experience moments in the limelight, and she wanted them to always remember the value of integrity and transparency. She used examples from her career to illustrate how important it was never to lose sight of their true selves, always staying connected to their roots and values. Her words, filled with sincerity, left a profound impact on her children, who saw her as a model of balance between ambition and humility.

Through these conversations, Kim conveyed not only life lessons but also deep, constant love, making her children feel part of her story and instilling in them the awareness that, despite life's challenges, they would always have the strength to fight their own battles. For her, sharing her experiences was a way to stay close to her children, ensuring each one felt loved and supported in finding their own path.

Providing Emotional Support at Every Stage

For Kim, emotional support was at the core of her role as a mother. She was convinced that each child, regardless of age or the challenges they faced, needed to know they had solid, unconditional support. With constant attention, Kim made sure to be there for her children in every phase of their growth, ready to offer comfort, advice, or simply a listening ear. She understood that each child had unique needs, and to build a strong bond, it was essential to understand their personalities and tailor her approach to their individual needs.

During difficult times, like the transition from childhood to adolescence, Kim was a reassuring presence. She encouraged her children to express their emotions freely, without fear of judgment, creating a space where they felt comfortable sharing their fears and doubts. This openness was especially important to her, knowing how rare it was, especially in the celebrity world, to have a space for true self-expression. Her words were always thoughtful, aimed at encouraging without imposing, showing them that every emotion was valid and that together they would find the right way forward.

In moments of insecurity, Kim helped her children see that even uncertain times could be growth opportunities. She taught them to view challenges as chances to build resilience and to appreciate the value of mutual support within the family. Whenever one of them faced an obstacle, Kim offered her own experiences, recounting how she had overcome similar situations. These shared moments, accompanied by gestures of affection and words of encouragement, strengthened the family bond.

Kim also emphasized the importance of mental well-being, reminding her children that emotional health was just as vital as physical health. If she noticed any of them feeling particularly pressured or stressed, she encouraged them to take a break, finding activities to help them relax and achieve balance. For her, creating a calm, stable environment was not only a priority but a mission, ensuring that her children knew they could always count on her.

Through this constant support, Kim not only offered emotional sustenance but also created a network of love that her children would carry with them throughout their lives. Her unconditional love and tireless presence provided a foundation on which each could build their future, knowing they would always have a safe harbor to return to.

Building a Bond Based on Trust and Open Communication

Kim built a bond with her children based on trust and open dialogue, two pillars she believed were essential to a strong family relationship. Every conversation, whether a simple evening chat or a deeper discussion, was an opportunity for her to strengthen their bond and teach them to express their ideas and emotions freely. Her goal was for her children to feel comfortable approaching her about anything, confident that they would be heard without judgment.

From an early age, Kim showed her children that dialogue was a two-way street: it wasn't just about giving advice but also about listening and understanding their experiences and perspectives. When they were young, she introduced a "story night," a weekly ritual where they would share experiences, dreams, and challenges. This practice continued as they grew older, providing a safe space for discussing complex topics as well. Through this ritual, Kim gained insight into her children's thoughts and aspirations, deepening her understanding of their inner emotions and providing the support they needed.

During adolescence, a period often marked by change and challenges, Kim's open communication took on even greater importance. She encouraged her children to share their worries without fear, assuring them that they would always find in her a supportive listener. When one of them faced a challenge, instead of simply providing an answer, Kim asked them to reflect and talk about their feelings, fostering emotional awareness and introspection.

The trust Kim built with them was so strong that, even in the most difficult moments, her children knew they could rely on her. She made them feel that their relationship was not based on expectations or conditions but on unconditional love. This certainty motivated them to open up, cultivating the same honesty and sincerity in their own relationships with others. They knew that, regardless of mistakes or obstacles, they would always find in Kim an understanding mother and a guide.

Through constant dialogue and mutual trust, Kim created a united family where every member felt valued and respected. This connection, founded on empathy and mutual support, continued to grow, forming the basis of a love destined to last a lifetime.

Chapter 13: The Relationship with Diddy: A Lasting Collaboration

A Bond Beyond Separation

Despite the end of their romantic relationship, Kim and Diddy managed to maintain a profound connection, built on respect and affection. With remarkable maturity, Kim chose to look beyond the pain and disappointments of Diddy's infidelities during their relationship, setting aside personal grievances to provide a serene, stable family environment for their children. For Kim, the separation wasn't just an ending but a new chapter. Although the experience had its share of challenges, she showed inner strength and generosity, refusing to let resentment overpower her.

Kim often suffered in silence, concealing her vulnerability to protect her children's well-being. Even when difficulties seemed insurmountable, she maintained a respectful attitude toward Diddy, acknowledging his role in the children's lives and prioritizing their emotional stability. Through remarkable responsibility, she cultivated a calm, collaborative relationship, demonstrating that family ties could endure personal wounds.

This maturity became the foundation of the co-parenting approach that Kim and Diddy developed. They recognized the importance of presenting a united front to offer their children a positive model of respect and cooperation. Kim understood that a peaceful home environment would help her children form a positive outlook on relationships, teaching them the value of respect and collaboration.

Over time, Kim and Diddy forged a partnership that extended beyond shared parenting responsibilities. They found a balance rooted in trust and mutual responsibility. Kim retained her independence while remaining a central figure in her children's lives, fostering a peaceful relationship with Diddy and acknowledging his role as their father. This enduring collaboration became, for their children, a tangible example of how love for family could overcome personal challenges with respect and unity.

Co-Parenting as a Priority

Following the end of their relationship, Kim and Diddy reached a fundamental agreement: to put their children's well-being first and provide them with a stable, peaceful environment. Although their lives were separate, they both remained committed to maintaining an authentic, ongoing partnership beyond any personal resentments. For Kim, co-parenting wasn't merely about sharing responsibilities but about being a constant, united presence for the children. Every decision they made prioritized the children's needs, building a model of collaboration that respected both parents' roles.

Despite personal challenges and demands, Kim ensured open communication and collaboration with Diddy on every decision regarding the children's well-being. Co-parenting required discipline and dedication that went beyond mere physical presence; it demanded building a steady, reliable guide for the children even within a separated family.

Kim was deeply committed to giving her children two fully supportive parents. Even during moments of tension, she worked to preserve a sense of harmony, avoiding conflict that might disrupt her children's peace. Her ability to maintain open, respectful communication with Diddy allowed her to overcome emotional barriers, solidifying a relationship that remained strong and family-centered.

Over time, this collaboration proved to be a mature, loving choice for the children, creating a supportive, stable environment. The co-parenting foundation that Kim and

Diddy built provided the children with a sense of security, showing them an example of mutual dedication and respect. Through this approach, Kim transformed a complex situation into a growth opportunity for the family, affirming that love for one's children could truly overcome personal challenges.

Shared Celebrations and Important Moments

Even after their relationship ended, Kim and Diddy understood the importance of being present together for their children during significant moments. Birthdays, holidays, school ceremonies—every special occasion was an opportunity to create positive memories and share family joy. Kim firmly believed that, despite the separation, it was essential to let the children feel that their family was united and that both parents were willing to set aside their differences to celebrate together.

Participating in these events often required a level of coordination and cooperation that wasn't easy to achieve. Kim, with her calm and respectful approach, ensured that each celebration was peaceful and enjoyable. She recognized the impact these gestures had on the children, who felt secure and protected seeing both parents together. These celebrations became not only moments of joy but also concrete demonstrations of Kim and Diddy's commitment to their children's happiness.

These shared moments, however brief, reinforced a sense of family unity and stability. Kim put her heart into making every occasion special for her children, paying attention to every detail and ensuring they felt cherished. During these events, she let the children be the center of attention, giving them the freedom to enjoy the moment. Her quiet presence, along with Diddy's support, created an atmosphere where the children could truly enjoy the celebration, without any sense of tension.

Over the years, these shared events became family rituals, tangible examples of how Kim and Diddy found a way to coexist harmoniously for their family's sake. Their side-by-side presence at these important moments confirmed to the children the strength of their family bond. Kim and Diddy showed that, even though they were no longer a couple, they would always be a safe and stable support for their children, demonstrating the lasting value of family.

Kim's Support During Diddy's Pressured Moments

Even after their romantic relationship ended, Kim continued to be a guiding presence for Diddy, especially during times when the public pressures and career challenges tested his stability. Kim understood the unpredictable nature of the entertainment industry and the difficulty of balancing success with personal life. With discretion and maturity, she remained a comforting presence for him during the most intense periods.

As a confidante and sincere friend, Kim was willing to listen without judgment and offer honest advice. When Diddy faced a crisis or stressful situation, he knew he could rely on her for a comforting word or a suggestion to help him find calm. With her inner strength and wisdom, Kim encouraged him to prioritize self-care and keep family at the center of his decisions.

This support involved sacrifices on Kim's part. She remained available and patient, even when their personal situation might have justified distancing herself. Kim was aware of Diddy's influence on their children's lives and understood that his well-being directly impacted their family's stability. Without reservation, she continued to offer her help when he needed it, nurturing a bond based on mutual respect and understanding.

Kim's support was more than just words; it was visible in her constant encouragement and small, thoughtful gestures. For the children, her willingness to maintain this relationship with Diddy showed the importance of cultivating a positive connection even after separation. Kim embodied the principle that respect and support should never fade, especially when shared responsibilities as parents are involved. Her example offered the children a valuable life lesson: the strength to set aside the past and continue supporting those they love for the sake of family and the love they once shared.

An Inclusive, Extended Family

Over time, Kim and Diddy created a family environment where each member felt welcome and valued, despite the complexities of a blended family structure. Kim fully understood the challenges this type of family presented, yet she approached each one with patience and understanding, working to ensure a sense of unity and belonging. Her priority was to create an environment where the children felt loved and supported, no matter the differences among them.

Kim's strength lay in her ability to include and unite. She constantly ensured each child felt appreciated and heard, emphasizing the family's value as a safe haven. Despite separations and difficulties, Kim wanted her children to grow up with a strong sense of belonging, nurtured not only in shared celebrations but also in the everyday. For her, building an extended family meant teaching her children the importance of empathy and solidarity, values that went beyond biological ties.

This inclusive approach was evident in small gestures: family dinners, group outings, or heartfelt conversations where each family member could freely express themselves. Kim encouraged her children to view their siblings as close companions, helping them realize they were part of a family rooted in love and mutual respect. Her actions offered the children a model of how to embrace differences and build authentic bonds.

This inclusive atmosphere allowed the children to grow up in a conflict-free, rivalry-free environment, where each felt part of a shared mission. Kim and Diddy, despite no longer being romantically involved, collaborated to ensure each family member found their place and was respected. Through this, their children learned that family could be a source of strength and stability, welcoming and protecting without prejudice or limits. For Kim, this was the ultimate achievement of her role as a mother: creating a bond that transcended all distinctions, offering her children a truly united family.

Recognizing Each Other's Contributions

Despite the challenges that marked their relationship, Kim and Diddy built a rapport based on deep respect for each other's roles and efforts within the family. Kim appreciated Diddy's commitment to being present in their children's lives, even when work took him away. In turn, Diddy saw in Kim a stable, reliable figure, a loving mother who was the family's heart and dedicatedly cared for their children.

This mutual respect wasn't something taken for granted; it required awareness and maturity. Kim understood the challenges and pressures Diddy faced in the entertainment world, which she herself knew well and which often tested family ties. For this reason, she never missed an opportunity to acknowledge his efforts, showing gratitude for the dedication with which he sought to build a strong bond with their children despite his professional demands.

Diddy, on the other hand, recognized the sacrifices involved in raising four children, especially with such public exposure.

He admired Kim's role in maintaining the family's balance and appreciated her ability to be both mother and guide, a constant presence in the children's lives. This mutual respect transformed into constructive dialogue, where they shared experiences and concerns, aware that their combined efforts aimed at one shared goal: their children's peace and happiness.

For their children, witnessing their parents' mutual appreciation provided a valuable example of overcoming differences and creating relationships based on understanding and respect. Through their attitude, Kim and Diddy showed that even in a non-traditional family setup, love for one's family can be a solid, sincere foundation capable of inspiring and teaching gratitude and generosity.

Supporting Their Children's Projects and Ambitions

Both parents shared a fundamental value: the desire to see their children grow up free to explore their passions and ambitions. This common goal brought them together to support each child's aspirations with encouragement and attentiveness. With an approach based on understanding each child's unique interests, they worked together to ensure their children faced the world with confidence, knowing they always had someone by their side.

Quincy, the eldest, showed a strong inclination toward acting and music, following in his adoptive father's footsteps. With her steady, attentive nature, Kim encouraged him to participate in projects that reflected his values and talent. Diddy, knowing the nuances of the entertainment industry, provided valuable advice, teaching Quincy to handle challenges with professionalism and self-respect. Together, they created an environment where Quincy could express himself freely and find his voice.

Christian, with his charisma and natural talent for fashion, was drawn to the field where Kim had started her career. Aware of the industry's challenges, she instilled in him the importance of perseverance and authenticity, urging him to remain true to himself. Diddy, meanwhile, encouraged Christian to explore music as well, sharing his passion for creative work and the responsibility it entails. Together, they presented him with various paths, knowing the importance of building a meaningful and resilient career.

Even the twins, D'Lila Star and Jessie James, began to show signs of curiosity and talent, admiring both their mother and father. With great care, Kim nurtured their creative spirit, encouraging them to explore interests that they could develop over time. While protecting the two young girls to some degree, both Kim and Diddy were enthusiastic about watching them grow up in an environment where they could pursue their interests without pressure, experimenting and discovering what made them unique.

In this environment, their support represented a foundation of unconditional love and freedom. Kim and Diddy showed them how to pursue dreams with commitment and passion without sacrificing authenticity. Their encouragement was sincere and profound, rooted in the intention to allow the children the freedom to be themselves. This approach conveyed a valuable message: in life, true fulfillment comes from following one's heart, knowing one has a family that believes in their potential.

A Model of Respect for Their Children

Kim and Diddy, despite the challenges they faced over the years, turned their experience into a positive example for their children, demonstrating that respect can transcend personal differences and past conflicts. Kim, with her maturity and composure, never allowed herself to be overwhelmed by resentment over the past difficulties with Diddy. Instead, she presented her children with an authentic yet peaceful view of family life, emphasizing that integrity and the ability to forgive are essential to strengthening bonds.

On various occasions, Kim shared reflections with Quincy, Christian, and the twins on the values of dignity and patience. She tried to make them understand that even during challenging moments, it was vital to never lose their authenticity, teaching them that inner strength comes from preserving one's identity and dignity. For his part, Diddy conveyed to the children the importance of gratitude toward those who shared a meaningful journey, helping them understand that love doesn't fade with separation but can evolve into mutual respect and support.

During hectic times, such as moments of media exposure or public tension, Kim made every effort to shield her children from the pressure, carefully choosing words and moments for dialogue. She emphasized the importance of focusing on people's positive qualities rather than dwelling on past mistakes, encouraging her children to find lessons for growth in every experience.

This life perspective that Kim and Diddy conveyed to their children, grounded in values like resilience and humanity, taught them that every human relationship, even the most complex, can bring value when approached with respect and maturity. For the children, witnessing their parents' cooperation and mutual appreciation was more than a lesson—it was a tangible guide to building strong, respectful relationships.

DISCOVER THE HEART AND LEGACY OF KIM PORTER

Scan the QR code to explore an exclusive collection of Kim's most meaningful moments: **a heartfelt photo album, a detailed timeline, and a commemorative video that honor her light and impact.** Get to know Kim not just as an icon, but as an extraordinary woman

t.ly/GKMju

Chapter 14: Public Criticism and Charitable Initiatives

Life Under the Spotlight

Being connected to a high-profile figure like Diddy inevitably brought Kim into the public eye, making her private life a subject of public interest. Every step, choice, or appearance was scrutinized and analyzed by the media and fans, often with an intensity and criticism that could challenge even the strongest individuals. Despite this, Kim maintained an unwavering sense of self, displaying a calm and balanced approach to the challenges of fame.

This visibility, while at times an advantage for her career, also came with pressures that could be challenging to manage. Every decision, statement, and personal relationship was subject to public judgment, making it difficult to maintain a sense of normalcy for herself and, more importantly, for her children. Kim frequently navigated the fine line between being a public figure and her desire to protect her family and relationships from external intrusion.

However, her approach to fame was marked by calm and authenticity that captivated everyone who encountered her. Kim avoided flashy behaviors and dramatic tones, opting instead to face her visibility with disarming naturalness. Her discreet and reassuring presence communicated elegance and integrity, allowing her to build a deep connection with the public beyond her association with Diddy. Her life under the spotlight was characterized by a constant focus on essential values such as family and personal dignity.

Being consistently under the media's critical eye also meant managing her emotions and maintaining a coherent self-image. Kim did this while staying true to herself, representing a strong and authentic woman who handled fame with a grounded inner balance. Her example inspired many, proving that public success should never compromise a person's essence.

Handling Criticism with Grace and Calm

Over the years, Kim developed a unique resilience in dealing with the criticism and judgments that inevitably accompanied her life in the spotlight. Aware that as a public figure she would be subject to opinions of all kinds—sometimes unjust or based on misunderstandings—she chose to respond to every comment with grace and calm, demonstrating an inner strength that did not go unnoticed.

Kim learned to separate her self-worth from external opinions, adopting a detached stance that allowed her to remain unaffected by negativity. This ability was not innate but developed over time as a response to the challenges fame brought her way. Her approach was simple yet effective: to maintain her balance and focus on what truly mattered, like her family, projects, and supporters. She understood that criticism could be fleeting and that what truly mattered was staying true to herself.

For many women, especially those in the entertainment industry, maintaining composure in the face of negative comments can be a significant challenge, but Kim was an exception. She faced every situation with a measured demeanor, reflecting rare wisdom and becoming a role model for others facing similar pressures. Her calm reactions and ability to avoid public conflict allowed her to build a solid image based on respect and integrity.

Her ability to remain calm and avoid impulsive reactions to what was said or written about her was a reflection of profound self-awareness. Kim knew that each challenge and comment was an opportunity to grow and strengthen herself, teaching her children the value of not letting others define their self-worth. Her grace under criticism added an aura of elegance and wisdom, inspiring many to follow her example.

Support from Family and Friends

Despite fame and life under the spotlight, Kim always stayed close to her family and dear friends, who were her anchor and strength in times of difficulty. Surrounded by people who knew her as the woman she was beyond the celebrity, she found in them a safe haven and invaluable emotional support. This deep connection with loved ones served as her grounding, helping her stay centered even amid the challenges of fame.

Kim had an extraordinary ability to maintain genuine relationships despite her success. Her sincere character and open-hearted nature made it easy for friends and family to love her unconditionally. For Kim, it was important not only to receive support but also to give it. She frequently showed her gratitude to those close to her with sincere gestures of affection, building relationships based on loyalty, respect, and mutual trust.

In moments of heightened pressure, such as when the media scrutinized her personal life or she faced unfair criticism, the closeness of her loved ones was crucial. Kim drew strength from friends who understood her struggles and supported her without judgment. She could openly confide in them, sharing anxieties and concerns and also celebrating her joys and successes, creating a space where she could express herself without fearing public judgment.

This circle of loved ones served as an example for her children, who saw how essential it was to build solid and sincere relationships. Kim encouraged them to surround themselves with people who offered support and to form bonds based on authentic values. Her ability to accept and return the support of those who cared for her was one of the qualities that made her unique, further demonstrating her humility and love for those in her life.

Charitable Initiatives as an Expression of Authenticity

For Kim, the desire to do good was an authentic calling, an aspect of her personality that went beyond merely participating in charitable causes. Her initiatives reflected deep values she had always cultivated: respect, empathy, and the belief that everyone could make a difference in the lives of others. Her commitment to social causes wasn't just for the public eye but was a genuine way of expressing who she was.

Among the causes closest to her heart were those dedicated to supporting young people in need, with a particular focus on women and children. Kim actively collaborated with organizations in New York, the city she considered home, participating in fundraisers and supporting educational programs to promote the well-being of underprivileged families. She deeply believed in the power of solidarity and the role of the community as a resource for facing life's challenges.

One of her favorite causes was supporting young women by providing them with educational resources and psychological support to help them build independent futures. Kim often shared her life experiences as a testament to resilience and determination, participating in charitable events not just as a celebrity but as a genuine woman eager to make a difference.

She was actively involved in charity events around the city, using her visibility to raise awareness of causes close to her heart and helping to raise funds for family-centered programs. Despite her fame, she was always willing to stay in the background, allowing the concrete results of the initiatives she supported to take center stage.

Kim's dedication to social causes was a way for her to remain true to her values and convey a message of hope and change— not only to her children but to everyone she encountered. Her generosity extended beyond public gestures; each contribution was part of a broader vision of life where every act of kindness truly mattered.

Balancing Public and Private Life

Kim Porter possessed a rare ability to maintain a balanced approach to her public and private life, a valuable talent that helped her navigate the most complex moments of her life in the spotlight. Despite the visibility and constant pressures of the entertainment world, Kim managed to build an authentic and peaceful life where family and personal values remained central to her choices.

The secret to this balance lay in her ability to set clear boundaries between her personal life and public obligations. Over time, she learned to handle moments of notoriety without being overwhelmed, ensuring that criticisms or external expectations didn't affect her self-perception. Her maturity led her to a life where fame didn't define her worth but became a means to achieve more meaningful goals.

She was deeply aware of the importance of protecting her children's peace of mind, creating a family environment where they could feel safe and shielded from external tensions. Despite constant media attention, she managed to build a space filled with love and tranquility, where her children could grow without being subjected to the pressures of the public eye. Kim gracefully balanced her desire to be part of their daily lives with her determination to protect them from the shadows fame could bring.

For her, balance also meant knowing when to take a break and focus on herself, allowing her to recharge and face new challenges with serenity. This ability to prioritize her well-being enabled her to be a present mother and an authentic individual, able to handle responsibilities with awareness and inner strength. Those who knew her described her as a rare soul, someone who could live with grace and determination even in challenging times.

Her example was a precious model for everyone who knew her, inspiring those around her to find their way to balance personal life and ambitions. Kim showed that, even in the entertainment industry, it was possible to stay true to oneself and one's values—a message she continued to leave as a legacy for anyone inspired by her story. This carefully cultivated balance was the key that allowed her to face every challenge with strength and peace of mind.

Chapter 15: The Tragedy of Kim's Passing

A Day of Pain and Disbelief

On November 15, 2018, the world came to a standstill for everyone who loved Kim Porter. News of her passing struck like a thunderbolt on a clear day, leaving family, friends, and fans in profound shock and disbelief. It was unimaginable that someone so full of life and light could depart so suddenly and without warning. It was as if the heart of her family—the core of love that Kim had so carefully and devotedly built—had ceased to beat.

Diddy, devastated by the loss of the woman he called his "soulmate," found himself revisiting the memories they shared, the smiles, the laughter, and the challenges they had faced together. The disbelief shadowed him, and every thought of her felt almost unreal. Her children, suddenly deprived of their greatest guide and support, felt lost, as if an irreplaceable piece of their lives had been torn away. The home that once echoed with her laughter now lay silent, a silence that was deafening.

On social media, a torrent of love filled the pages dedicated to Kim: friends, colleagues, and fans shared thoughts, memories, moments spent together, or simply spoke of the inspiration they drew from her. From all corners of the world, everyday people and celebrities united in grief, bearing witness to the enormous impact Kim had had on their lives. That day became a symbol of collective pain, where every message, every word, was a final farewell to a woman who had profoundly touched the hearts of all who knew her.

Kim had been a beacon of hope and love. And, though that day was one of the darkest, those who loved her knew her light would continue to shine through memories, giving them the strength to carry on, even when it seemed impossible.

The Cause of Death and Initial Investigations

Kim's tragic passing left a wave of questions and uncertainties about what had truly caused her sudden death. The news hit her family, friends, and fans worldwide with a profound impact as the media reported the first official details. Initial reports suggested cardiac arrest, but further investigations pointed to lobar pneumonia as the cause of death—a diagnosis that surprised many given Kim's young age and seemingly robust health.

In the days leading up to her death, Kim had shown signs of illness, complaining of fever, sweats, and flu-like symptoms. According to family members, she had also experienced severe pain and fatigue, displaying symptoms that initially appeared to be nothing more than seasonal flu. Despite medical assistance and the attention of her loved ones, her condition deteriorated rapidly, leading to a premature and heartbreaking end.

The autopsy revealed a clear diagnosis: pneumonia had invaded her lung tissue, causing a severe infection that led to respiratory failure. The initial investigation was conducted by the Los Angeles County Medical Examiner-Coroner, who confirmed the findings a few days after Kim's passing, addressing social media speculation and providing an official explanation for the cause of her death. However, despite these statements, the public continued to express skepticism, as the news of her death had been so sudden and unexpected.

For her family, especially her children and Diddy, accepting this medical reality was a painful and difficult step. While the world sought answers through articles and news reports, every piece of information for them carried a heavy weight, making the heartbreaking loss all the more real.

Grief Among Family and Friends

News of Kim Porter's passing left an open wound not only within her family but also among her friends and colleagues in the entertainment world. Among the first to publicly express their sorrow was Diddy, who shared a heartfelt message on social media dedicated to Kim, remembering her as a woman with a tremendous heart and a devoted mother capable of offering unconditional love to everyone who entered her life. His grief was not only that of an ex-partner but of a man deeply grateful for the legacy of love Kim had left, one she had built with strength and dedication, creating a solid family united by profound values.

Kim's children, devastated by the loss, also chose to remember her with words full of love and gratitude. Quincy, her firstborn, spoke of her as a guide and a source of inspiration, while Christian and the twins, D'Lila Star and Jessie James, found the strength to honor her memory through shared family moments, preserving the image of a present and loving mother.

Besides her family, numerous friends and celebrities publicly expressed their grief. Icons from the music and fashion world, like Mary J. Blige and Missy Elliott, remembered Kim for her natural elegance, her generosity, and her ever-bright spirit. For many of her friends, Kim's passing also led to reflection on the importance of resilience and mutual support among women— values Kim herself embodied.

The public mourning sparked a series of spontaneous commemorations, with friends and colleagues sharing memories and messages on social media. Among these was a private ceremony organized by Diddy, gathering close family and friends to honor Kim's memory in a respectful, intimate atmosphere. During the ceremony, anecdotes and stories were shared, allowing those present to relive the best moments spent with Kim, keeping her memory alive through the testimonies of those who loved and deeply appreciated her.

Her absence continues to be felt as an irreparable void, but the words and actions of those who knew her are a testament to the indelible mark she left behind. Kim Porter was not only a mother and partner but also a figure who knew how to inspire strength and hope in people—a quality that made her memory a symbol of love and resilience.

Diddy's Farewell: Words of Love and Remembrance

Kim's passing was a devastating loss for Diddy, who, despite the end of their romantic relationship, continued to hold a deep affection for her. After the tragedy, Diddy shared a public tribute in which he expressed with touching words the emptiness left by his ex-partner and the mother of his children, describing his love and gratitude for the time they had spent together.

During the funeral ceremony in Georgia, Diddy's farewell was filled with emotion. As he recalled the small daily gestures and experiences they shared as a couple and as parents, he painted an intimate portrait of their relationship, highlighting the beauty of the bond that had united them. The moving stories of Kim's dedication as a mother and her strength as a woman echoed as a tribute to her memory, creating a deeply emotional atmosphere among all present.

For fans and those who knew them, Diddy's tribute was a testament to a rare connection that transcended challenges and time. His promise to continue honoring Kim as he raised their children was a lasting commitment—a symbol of the unconditional love that endures even after loss. Thus, the ceremony became not only a moment of farewell but a celebration of Kim's life and legacy, which would forever accompany her family.

Public Commemoration and Fans' Outpouring of Love

Kim Porter's loss deeply affected not only her family but also a vast community of friends and fans who had followed her life and career. In the days following her passing, social media platforms were flooded with messages of condolences and affection. Celebrities, colleagues, and acquaintances shared memories and personal anecdotes, creating a collective tribute that celebrated Kim's positive impact on their lives.

Fans paid tribute to Kim's memory with spontaneous commemorations in various cities, including New York and Atlanta. Some organized vigils and gatherings to honor her, lighting candles and sharing stories about how her life had inspired them. The image of Kim as a strong, loving, and genuine woman remained etched in the hearts of many, who saw her as an example of resilience and dignity.

In Los Angeles, where Kim had spent much of her life, an official commemoration was organized, attended by close friends and personalities from the entertainment industry. During the ceremony, a video montage displayed special images and moments from her life, highlighting her generous spirit and dedication to her family. The tribute culminated in heartfelt words from her children and close friends, who remembered her as a caring mother, a sincere friend, and a source of inspiration.

The fans' outpouring of love continued even months after her passing, with online initiatives celebrating her memory. Some created foundations and fundraising campaigns in her name, supporting causes Kim would surely have championed. Her legacy continued to live on through those who loved and respected her, uniting the hearts of those who felt they had lost a special presence.

An Absence That Changes Everything

Kim's passing left an irreplaceable void in the lives of her family, her friends, and everyone who knew her. Her children suddenly faced the reality of life without their mother's daily support—a figure who had been the cornerstone of family life. However, this void became, for each of them, a reason to rediscover the values and lessons Kim had imparted, keeping her spirit alive through memories and bonds of affection built over time.

For Diddy, who had shared joys and hardships with Kim for years, her memory became a new source of inspiration. Although their romantic relationship had ended long before her death, the emotional and familial bond that united them remained strong. Diddy committed to doing everything possible to maintain family stability and provide his children with the support they needed to cope with the loss. His words during the official commemoration made it clear how deeply he loved Kim—a love that would forever remain alive in the heart of their family.

For her children, Kim's absence became a push to honor her memory by following in her footsteps and upholding her teachings. Each of them, in their own way, sought to keep her legacy alive, whether by dedicating themselves to charitable causes, as Kim had always done, or drawing from her strength and resilience to face their own challenges. The twin sisters, although very young, felt the importance of their connection to their mother through stories and memories shared by family, fostering a sense of belonging and love that transcended physical separation.

Over time, Kim's absence became not just a memory of pain but also a symbol of strength for her family. Her spirit continued to live on through her children and those who loved her, inspiring a new generation to follow her example of generosity and courage.

Chapter 16: Conspiracy Theories and Speculation about Kim Porter's Death

The Start of Online Speculation

The news of Kim's passing sparked an outpouring of grief, followed, unfortunately, by a surge of online speculation. On social media and various forums, voices began questioning the official cause of death, attributed to lobar pneumonia. Some individuals, driven by sorrow and disbelief, began formulating conspiracy theories that suggested Kim may have been a victim of dark circumstances or even foul play. The speed with which these theories spread reflects the modern tendency of social media to amplify speculation and make content based on hypotheses rather than facts go viral.

These speculations were fueled by a series of posts on popular platforms such as Twitter and Reddit, where some users claimed that Kim's public figure status and her connections in the music and entertainment industry might have played a role in her death. Users pointed to the scant details initially released to the press, insinuating that there was more to the official explanation. In some cases, these theories drew on past events or urban legends already circulating in the entertainment world, connecting them in arbitrary ways and spreading unverified information that only added to public confusion.

In response, Kim's family and friends sought to maintain their privacy and observe a period of mourning, hoping that the wave of unfounded theories would subside. However, the rapid spread of these ideas generated growing media pressure on the family, already shaken by grief. This episode became a sad example of how online platforms can amplify misinformation, adding to the suffering of those left behind.

Statements from Family and Friends

In response to the spread of conspiracy theories and a controversial memoir, Kim Porter's family decided to take a public stance to defend her memory and put an end to the falsehoods. Kim's children released a joint statement expressing their pain at the exploitation of their mother's passing and reiterating the official cause of death: Kim had passed due to lobar pneumonia, a well-documented medical condition confirmed by health authorities. The family's statement emphasized that there was no evidence of foul play or suspicious circumstances, calling for respect for Kim and the pain caused by her loss.

Diddy, who had shared significant years of his life with Kim, joined the family's voice, making statements filled with affection and respect for her memory. On multiple occasions, he publicly spoke of how she had been a fundamental presence in his life and how her passing had left an unfillable void. In a heartfelt and respectful tone, Diddy sought to dispel any suspicions surrounding her death, focusing on memories of Kim's qualities, such as her strength, her love for family, and her generosity.

Friends of Kim, including well-known faces in the entertainment industry, shared messages of support and affection for the family, expressing disdain for the baseless rumors. Each statement painted a picture of a beloved and respected woman, whose loss deserved to be remembered for the positive impact she had on those who knew her, not for unfounded speculation. The goal of these statements was clear: to re-establish the truth and honor Kim for her life and legacy, not for baseless rumors.

The Impact of Conspiracy Theories on Public Opinion

The spread of conspiracy theories surrounding Kim Porter's death did not go unnoticed by the public, causing mixed reactions and fueling a debate that went far beyond the personal event. Despite official denials from the family and medical authorities, many continued to question the circumstances of her passing, unable to accept that such a beloved figure could depart due to natural causes. Social media, in particular, became a breeding ground for unverified hypotheses, with posts and discussions that ceaselessly speculated on possible backstories, often involving Kim's family directly.

The effect of these unfounded rumors was felt not only by those directly involved but also by Kim's public image and her legacy. Friends, colleagues, and fans found themselves defending Kim's memory from insinuations and suspicions, trying to refocus attention on what she had represented in life. The conspiracy theories managed to fuel a parallel narrative in which the truth was often obscured by the emotion of the moment and the lure of sensational stories.

This situation highlighted the importance of responsibility when dealing with information about people who have passed. The family themselves publicly expressed their pain not only over their loss but also over the devastating impact these speculations had on Kim's young, vulnerable children, who were now at the center of media attention. The conspiracy theories not only manipulated the truth but also ignored the respect owed to those mourning her. This episode underscored how misinformation can spread and create an alternate reality, leaving deep emotional wounds for those directly affected and turning the memory of a loved one into a media controversy.

The Removal of the Fake Book from Amazon

The release of a supposed memoir attributed to Kim Porter, titled *Kim's Lost Words: A Journey for Justice, from the Other Side*, immediately sparked outrage and concern. This book, which claimed to be an authentic account of Kim's life from her perspective, contained accusations and unfounded assertions about her death. Kim's family, deeply disturbed by the publication, publicly declared that the text had never been written or authorized by her. Her children openly denounced the work as a speculative venture aimed at exploiting their mother's name for commercial gain.

The pressure and protests from the family and fans led Amazon to remove the book from sale. This decision was welcomed as an important stand against unsubstantiated speculations. Amazon's choice to pull the work was seen as a gesture of respect for Kim's memory and an acknowledgment of the sensitivity of a situation still deeply painful for her loved ones. This episode highlighted the need for stricter publication controls and greater respect for the deceased and their families.

For Kim's family, Amazon's removal of the book was a moral victory and an example of how public opinion can help counter falsified narratives. However, despite the removal, the damage was already evident: Kim's memory had been manipulated, and many readers had been led to believe unverified information. This experience underscores the importance of an ethical and respectful approach when dealing with tragic events and the memory of loved ones, reminding us that respect for truth and family bonds should always come first.

The Importance of Verifying Sources and Respecting the Memory of the Deceased

The story of speculation surrounding Kim Porter's death and the publication of the fake memoir highlighted a delicate issue: the importance of always verifying sources and respecting the memory of those no longer with us. In an era where information can spread instantly, safeguarding the integrity of news becomes crucial, especially in cases of tragic events involving beloved figures. For Kim's family, the pain of their loss was further compounded by the false narratives circulating on social media and by irresponsible publications that distorted the truth and fueled unnecessary suspicions.

The spread of theories unsupported by concrete evidence not only leads to misunderstandings but can also cause deep wounds for those left behind. Kim's children repeatedly emphasized the importance of honoring the truth about their mother's death, calling for an empathetic and respectful approach to their loss. For them, Kim's memory should be honored not with speculation but with respect and a sincere remembrance of her life and positive impact.

This case highlights how essential source verification and respect are in preventing events and people from being manipulated for sensationalistic purposes. Honoring a life means remembering with love, avoiding unfounded accusations, and promoting the truth. Kim Porter deserved to be remembered for her strength, her love for her family, and her resilience. With this awareness, friends, fans, and family continue to keep her memory alive in an authentic way, showing that, even in the face of speculation, the value of truth and respect can prevail.

Chapter 17: Diddy's Musical Tribute to Kim Porter in 2023

The Decision to Honor Kim Porter at the VMAs

In September 2023, Diddy made a deeply significant choice: to honor his former partner and the mother of three of his children during his performance at the MTV Video Music Awards (VMAs). Dedicating part of the evening to her was more than a tribute to the woman who had been a cornerstone of his life; it was also a way to publicly face his grief and remember her indelible impact on his life and their children's lives. Kim's passing in 2018 left a profound void, one that Diddy aimed to fill through a commemorative gesture at a venue where music and emotion intersect.

This choice wasn't random. Diddy explained that performing with his son Christian "King" Combs was a dream Kim had often expressed. Bringing this dream to life on a global stage like the VMAs not only honored Kim but also represented a family reunion, underscoring the importance of the father-son bond.

In preparing for the event, father and son collaborated on every detail, carefully selecting songs that reflected both Diddy's artistic career and Kim's memory. The VMAs platform was an ideal setting, offering widespread visibility for sharing Kim's legacy and the lasting impact she left on those who knew and loved her. This collaboration gave Christian a space to showcase his talent and symbolized the strength of their familial love.

The tribute was received warmly by the audience, who felt the emotional intensity of the moment and the depth of this gesture. Many spectators and fans expressed their support and emotion on social media, showing that Kim's memory is still vibrant in popular culture. Through this tribute, Diddy demonstrated how love and respect for a cherished person can transcend time, inspiring others to remember and honor those they've lost.

An Emotional Performance with Christian "King" Combs

When Diddy decided to share the stage with his son Christian during the 2023 VMAs, it became a profoundly moving and emotional moment. For Diddy, the performance wasn't merely an expression of his talent but a chance to intertwine their artistic and personal lives, creating a tangible link between past and present, between father and son. Kim's absence, though painful, was transformed into a powerful presence, honoring her in an unforgettable way.

Christian, a young artist following in his father's footsteps, delivered an intense performance, demonstrating both his talent and the legacy his mother had left him. In that context, every lyric, every movement became a message of love and respect, a tribute that went beyond a mere musical performance. Diddy's presence beside him strengthened the significance of the performance, symbolizing a passing of the torch and a symbolic embrace of Kim's memory.

The intense glances exchanged between father and son, their perfect chemistry, and the energy they exuded conveyed to the audience the immense love that binds them. Christian was able to bring his personality and dedication to the stage, making his father proud and feeling that his mother was somehow watching over them. The performance thus became a family celebration, harmonizing music, talent, and memories.

The visibly moved fans and audience felt the depth of the moment and were swept away by the energy of the tribute. Through that tribute, Diddy and Christian offered the world a testament of resilience, love, and respect, showing that, despite loss, Kim's legacy continued to live on in them.

Diddy's Words in Memory of Kim

At the end of the performance, Diddy took a few moments to publicly share his love and respect for Kim, a woman who had left an indelible mark on his life. His voice heavy with emotion, he spoke with deep affection, describing Kim as a special person whose light continued to illuminate his family, even in her absence. His words were not just a tribute to a beloved partner and mother but an act of vulnerability in front of the world, expressing how profoundly he had been transformed by their bond.

Diddy spoke of their deep connection, one that neither time nor distance could sever. He said that Kim was a crucial part of his heart, a person who had always inspired his growth and sense of responsibility. He recounted how she had been a guide and source of stability, reminding the audience of her strength and courage in facing personal and professional challenges. His words filled the room with a solemn silence as each spectator shared in the pain and celebration of an extraordinary life.

The sincerity of his words deeply touched the audience, who felt the delicacy of that memory and the respect he held for her. By acknowledging Kim's support for his career and their family life, Diddy paid homage to a woman whose love and sacrifice had shaped his existence. His words were a tribute to Kim's strength, not only as a mother and partner but as a person whose lasting legacy and example would live on in their children and in him.

The Tribute's Impact on the Audience and Fans

The tribute left a lasting impression not only on those present at the VMAs but also on thousands of fans worldwide, who connected through broadcasts and social media. The intensity of the performance and Diddy's words in memory of Kim stirred a wave of emotion. Many spectators, friends, and supporters shared their reactions on social media, describing the tribute as an authentic, touching moment that transcended entertainment. It was an episode in which Diddy's personal reality intertwined with the public, revealing the more human side of a man known for success but now showing vulnerability and transparency.

The tribute sparked an emotional chain reaction, especially among Kim's fans, who felt part of a collective homage to her memory. Countless posts celebrated the love that Kim represented, praising her beauty, her spirit, and the way she had touched the lives of those who knew her. Her image shone once more in everyone's eyes, reminding them that her presence extended beyond her earthly life. The tribute offered fans a chance to unite in a common reflection on the resilience of love and the ability to preserve the memory of loved ones through both small and grand gestures.

This public commemoration also had a meaningful impact on the artistic community, inspiring artists, singers, and colleagues to reflect on the complexities of public life and the personal sacrifices it often entails. The respectful remembrance of Kim highlighted her positive legacy and her ability to remain a role model despite the challenges she faced. It was a tribute that allowed everyone not only to remember Kim but to recognize the value of love, family, and memory.

The impact of this celebration showed music and art's power to bring people together, revive precious moments, and keep alive the memories of those who are no longer with us. For Diddy and his children, that evening was more than a performance; it was a heartfelt tribute, offering them another

133

opportunity to keep their love for Kim alive and to let the world share in that eternal bond.

A Memory That Continues to Live in Pop Culture

The tribute was not only symbolic but a moment that solidified Kim's memory in pop culture. This gesture nourished a memory that was already vivid in the hearts of her fans and those close to her, cementing Kim's image as an icon not only for her contributions to the entertainment industry but also for the values she embodied as a woman, mother, and friend. Over the years, the affection for her has remained vivid, reflected in countless posts, messages, and tributes that friends, colleagues, and fans continue to share.

Diddy has played a key role in preserving Kim's legacy, ensuring that her memory extends beyond private family memories and into the public sphere. His words and Christian's presence on stage demonstrated how their love and respect for Kim is a palpable force, capable of enduring even beyond her passing. Pop culture has embraced Kim as a symbol of grace, resilience, and beauty, inspiring many who see her as an example of elegance and humanity.

Kim's legacy now intertwines with the worlds of music and entertainment. Like other icons who have left an indelible mark, such as Whitney Houston and Aaliyah, Kim Porter is remembered for her positive impact and the light she brought to the lives of everyone who knew her. Thanks to tributes like the one at the VMAs, her presence remains alive in contemporary culture, a symbol of eternal love and memories that transcend mortality.

For many, Kim now represents an example of unconditional love and inner strength. Her story, enriched by Diddy's tribute, has become a source of inspiration, continuing to illuminate the path of anyone who learns about her journey. Her memory, anchored in the hearts of her family and fans, remains a beacon for those who strive to face their challenges with dignity and grace.

Chapter 18: The 2024 Scandal: Diddy's Arrest

The Charges and Arrest in New York

On September 17, 2024, the arrest of Sean "Diddy" Combs became one of the year's most discussed events. The artist and entrepreneur was detained in New York on charges of organized crime and sex trafficking, sparking immense public interest and shock. The specific details of the charges were initially withheld from the public, but the case quickly drew media and fan attention, creating a significant rupture in the public perception of Diddy.

At the time of the arrest, authorities only released preliminary statements, confirming that the charges concerned grave allegations. The news surprised not only the entertainment world but also his family and friends, who initially chose to remain silent, likely to process the situation's implications. Known for his influence and mentorship to many artists, Diddy now found himself in a much different spotlight, one where his career and reputation were suddenly in jeopardy.

Law enforcement maintained a cautious approach, stating that, due to Diddy's high profile, all investigation details would be handled with the utmost respect for all involved. Following the arrest, restrictive measures were imposed on his travel, and Diddy's legal team quickly issued a statement asserting that he would fully cooperate with authorities to clarify all accusations. His lawyers emphasized that he was determined to defend his name and restore his integrity, underscoring that all involved deserved respectful treatment throughout the legal process.

The Reactions of Kim Porter's Family and Children

Diddy's arrest profoundly affected his family, especially the children he had with Kim Porter. The news not only generated a media storm but also added an emotional burden for

Christian, Quincy, D'Lila Star, and Jessie James, who were still coping with the early loss of their mother. The legal implications and accusations against their father created an emotionally challenging situation, especially with the public attention it garnered.

In the days following the arrest, the four children kept a low profile. Privacy and respect were prioritized, and no direct statements were released publicly. However, a few family members hinted at their reflections on social media, expressing messages that encouraged patience and mutual support, subtly suggesting the need for a measured approach.

Christian, active in the music industry, focused on his work and ongoing collaborations, maintaining a delicate balance between personal and professional life. Quincy, involved in entertainment, refrained from official statements, indicating his wish to manage this complex time privately. Meanwhile, the younger twins, D'Lila Star and Jessie James, were shielded from the media spotlight with the help of family and close friends.

Diddy's arrest and the family's reaction highlighted the importance of safeguarding the children's emotional stability as much as possible. Despite the challenges, Kim's family presented a united and resilient front, emphasizing the respect for the legal process and hoping for a clear outcome that would minimize further stress on the young family members involved. The priority remained maintaining emotional stability, shielding them from potential public repercussions, and striving for a semblance of normalcy amidst a difficult context.

Media Impact and Divided Public Opinion

The rapid spread of information intensified public opinion polarization. Many fans and industry colleagues spoke out in

Diddy's favor, invoking the presumption of innocence and emphasizing his lengthy track record of success and philanthropy. Numerous supporters voiced their hope that the charges would be refuted, recalling the positive impact Diddy had on many emerging artists and his contributions to charity projects.

At the same time, some segments of the public expressed skepticism, calling for transparency and clarity about the charges. For some, the revelations surrounding the arrest ignited a broader reflection on the music industry, often viewed as opaque and influenced by powerful interests. This division between unconditional supporters and critics reflected the growing debate on how celebrities are perceived, the boundaries between public and private life, and the responsibilities of prominent figures.

The incident also raised ethical questions about media exposure limits and the effects such high-profile cases can have on the private lives of family members and children.

Consequences for Diddy's Career and Project Suspensions

The arrest had immediate repercussions on Diddy's career and ongoing projects. Various commercial partnerships and sponsorships temporarily suspended their support, adopting a cautious stance as they awaited further legal developments. Some brands that had collaborated with Diddy for years issued statements reiterating the importance of awaiting justice while emphasizing transparency and respect for legal standards.

Television networks and streaming platforms reassessed certain projects involving Diddy, delaying their release to avoid compromising their image. Additionally, some scheduled music events saw adjustments, with organizers choosing to limit their association with an artist under investigation.

The impact on his business ventures highlighted the interdependence between public image and professional success. This period of uncertainty underscored how a delicate situation could prompt reconsideration from commercial partners, even for high-profile figures.

For Diddy, the project suspensions represent a setback that could have long-term repercussions, leaving the future of his career uncertain until the investigation concludes.

Prospects for the Trial and Kim's Legacy

As the legal situation evolves, future prospects carry crucial significance, not only for the legal implications but also for the emotional and familial repercussions. Kim's family, particularly her children, face this situation with resilience that reflects the legacy of strength she left behind. For them, their mother's memory represents a beacon of integrity and dignity, values they strive to uphold despite intense media exposure.

So far, the family's approach has been one of discretion, avoiding public comments and maintaining a low profile despite press attention and external pressures. This choice mirrors their respect for Kim's values, centered on love, dedication, and stability for her children's future. Their statements have been limited to expressing trust in the judicial system, underscoring the importance of focusing on what Kim would have wanted for them: a stable life grounded in family values.

Looking ahead, Kim's family remains committed to preserving her legacy, honoring her memory despite current challenges. This situation has strengthened family bonds, providing comfort and mutual support. While Diddy remains at the center of a public controversy, Kim's teachings endure, offering her loved ones guidance and an example of courage and compassion that help them face adversity.

Epilogue: Kim Porter's Legacy – A Life That Continues to Inspire

A Mother's Love and the Legacy of Family

Kim's love for her children was the very essence of her life—a force that transcended every challenge and circumstance. Family was at the heart of everything, and she cultivated an unbreakable bond with each of her children, imparting values that now live on in everything they do. Her four children learned from her the power of resilience, kindness, and sincerity—principles that guide them even in her absence. Kim was more than a mother; she was their guide, a constant presence who offered reassurance and support with a single glance or embrace.

Each child felt the deep love and dedication she poured into their growth. Kim's unique ability to respect each child's individuality while encouraging them to pursue their dreams—without ever sacrificing the values that held them together—continues to live on through them. This love manifests in their choices, their achievements, and the determination with which they face life.

Kim's legacy is more than a memory; it's a constant source of strength and inspiration—a thread that binds her memory to her children's future. Through her example, she showed them that true greatness lies not in fame or success, but in loving unconditionally and always being there for those they care about.

A Figure of Resilience and Grace

Kim moved through life with resilience that transcended hardship and a grace that uplifted everyone around her. Every challenge, from career highs and lows to personal complexities, was met with a dignity that left a lasting impression on those who knew her. Her unique blend of inner strength and authenticity allowed her to navigate difficulties while maintaining an elegant balance between public and private life.

Her grace extended to daily life, evident in the generosity with which she treated friends and the love she gave to her family. This genuine dedication shone through whenever she served as a beacon for her children and friends, showing them that it's possible to face adversity with integrity. Kim's resilience wasn't just an internal quality but a living lesson that continues to inspire those who remember her.

She left behind an example of living authentically, of someone who, despite challenges, chose the path of kindness and respect. This is her legacy—a timeless message of how strength can be expressed through gentleness and how grace can manifest even in the most trying moments.

Her Impact on Culture and the Entertainment Industry

With her unique style and natural talent, Kim left an indelible mark not only on fashion but also on pop culture and the entertainment industry. As a model, muse, and inspirational mother, she influenced generations, encouraging many to embrace their true selves and pursue their dreams with determination.

Her contributions to the industry were more than just her presence; she brought grace and depth to every project and collaboration. Over her career, she demonstrated the power of staying true to oneself in an environment often dominated by appearances and external pressures. Her example continues to resonate, becoming a source of inspiration for young artists and creatives who see in her a model of authenticity and resilience.

Beyond the spotlight, her ability to balance success with humanity sent a powerful message to the world: it's possible to excel while remaining true to one's values. Her legacy, therefore, extends beyond professional successes, living on in popular culture as a symbol of strength and sensitivity.

A Memory That Survives Hardships

Despite the challenges and hardships she faced, Kim's memory remains clear and powerful. The controversies that occasionally surrounded her family were unable to obscure the essence of who she truly was—a woman who lived with integrity, love, and extraordinary resilience. Everyone who knew her holds an image of Kim that transcends any scandal.

For her loved ones and fans, she remains an inspiring figure who transformed every difficulty into a life lesson. Now adults, her children carry her best qualities, reflecting the love and strength she instilled in them from childhood. Each milestone they reach, each brave choice they make, pays tribute to her memory and example.

Her legacy is not only a testament to success but a lesson in how to face hardships with dignity and courage. Kim's memory continues to shine, illuminating the path for those who had the privilege of knowing her and being inspired by her authenticity.

A Call to Remember Kim for Who She Truly Was

As this journey through Kim's life and memories comes to an end, what remains is not just the story of a successful woman but the portrait of an authentic and generous soul who transformed every encounter into something meaningful. Kim touched the lives of everyone she knew—not because of her public role but because of her ability to give of herself without reservation, to smile even in adversity, and to make others feel special.

I invite each reader to remember her for her warm smile, her deep love for her children, and her dedication to leaving the world a little better than she found it. Kim represents a model of love, resilience, and compassion—a woman who defied stereotypes and conventions to remain true to herself in every situation. In a world often driven by appearances, she chose authenticity, inspiring those close to her to do the same.

To remember Kim is to celebrate her love for life and the energy with which she approached each day. Her legacy lies not only in her achievements but in the values she instilled in her children and loved ones. Her memory is an invitation to live with purpose, courage, and to leave a trail of light for others.

In a rapidly changing world, may Kim's image remain a beacon of authenticity and inspiration. May her story continue to inspire those who hear it, showing that the greatest strength lies in the capacity to love, to be present, and to live every moment with truth and intensity.

Made in the USA
Columbia, SC
19 November 2024

47061600R00087